100 Songs in '30s

THE EASY THIRTIES FAKE BOOK

ISBN 978-1-4234-6390-0

HAL•LEONARD®
CORPORATION
7777 W. BLUEMOUND RD. P.O. BOX 13819 MILWAUKEE, WI 53213

Visit Hal Leonard Online at
www.halleonard.com

THE EASY THIRTIES FAKE BOOK

CONTENTS

INTRODUCTION

What Is a Fake Book?

A fake book has one-line music notation consisting of melody, lyrics and chord symbols. This lead sheet format is a "musical shorthand" that is an invaluable resource for all musicians—hobbyists to professionals.
Here's how *The Easy Thirties Fake Book* differs from most standard fake books:

- All songs are in the key of C.

- Many of the melodies have been simplified.

- Only five basic chord types are used—major, minor, seventh, diminished and augmented.

- The music notation is larger for ease of reading.

In the event that you haven't used chord symbols to create accompaniment, or your experience is limited, a chord speller chart is included at the back of the book to help you get started.

Have fun!

ALL OF ME

Words and Music by SEYMOUR SIMONS
and GERALD MARKS

ALL THE THINGS YOU ARE

from VERY WARM FOR MAY

Lyrics by OSCAR HAMMERSTEIN II
Music by JEROME KERN

Moderately

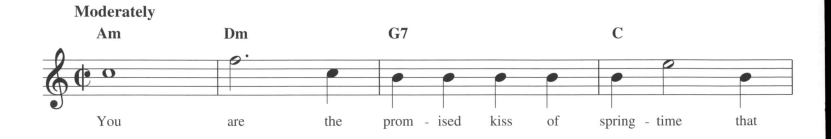

You are the prom - ised kiss of spring - time that

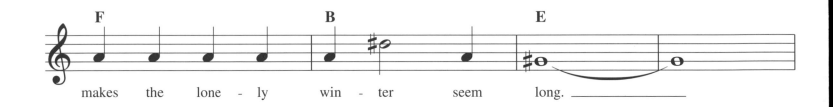

makes the lone - ly win - ter seem long. _____

You are the breath - less hush of eve - ning that

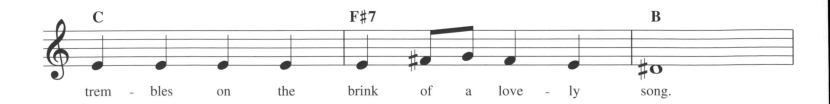

trem - bles on the brink of a love - ly song.

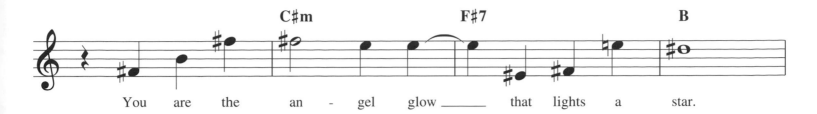

You are the an - gel glow _____ that lights a star.

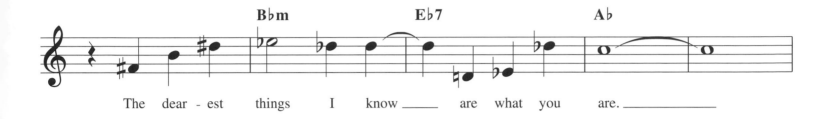

The dear - est things I know _____ are what you are. _____

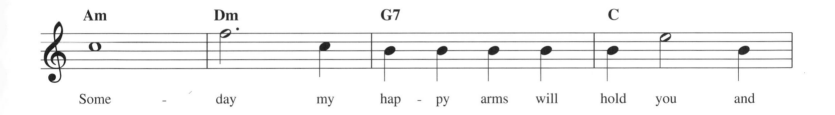

Some - day my hap - py arms will hold you and

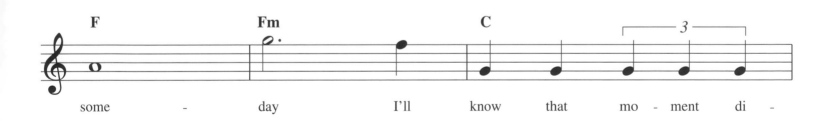

some - day I'll know that mo - ment di -

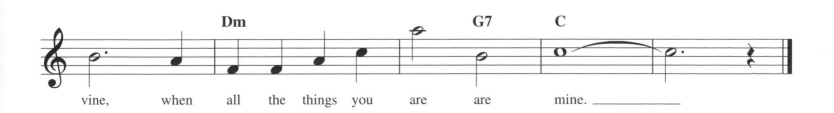

vine, when all the things you are are mine. _____

ARE YOU HAVIN' ANY FUN?
from GEORGE WHITE'S SCANDALS (1939 Edition)

Words by JACK YELLEN
Music by SAMMY FAIN

Moderately bright

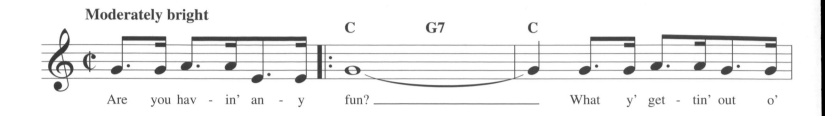

Are you hav - in' an - y fun? _____ What y' get - tin' out o'

liv - in'? ___ What good is what you've got ___ if you're

not hav - in' an - y fun? _____ Are you hav - in' an - y

laughs? _____ Are you get - tin' an - y lov - in'? _____

_____ If oth - er peo - ple do ___ so can you; have a lit - tle

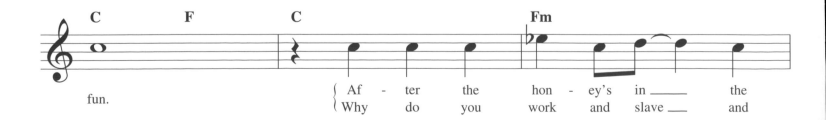

fun.   { Af - ter the hon - ey's in _____ the
         { Why do you work and slave ___ and

comb _____ lit - tle bees go out and play. _____ E - ven the
save? _____ Life is full of ifs and buts. _____ You know the

old grey mare down home _____ has got to have hay.
squir - rels save and save, _____ and what have they got?

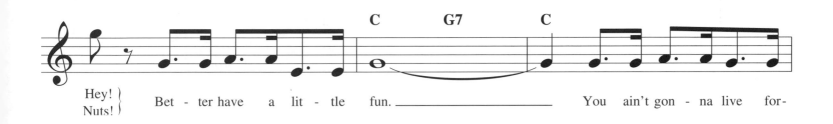

Hey! } Bet - ter have a lit - tle fun. _____ You ain't gon - na live for-
Nuts! }

ev - er. _____ Be - fore you're old and gray _____

still o - kay. _____ Have your lit - tle fun, son!

Have your lit - tle fun! Are you hav - in' an - y fun!

AUTUMN IN NEW YORK

Words and Music by
VERNON DUKE

With a lilt

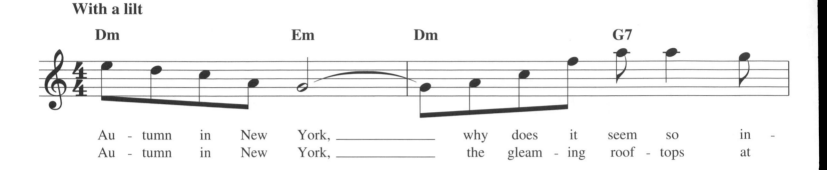

Au - tumn in New York, _____ why does it seem so in -
Au - tumn in New York, _____ the gleam - ing roof - tops at

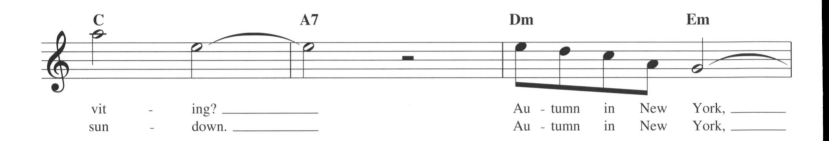

vit - ing? _____ Au - tumn in New York, _____
sun - down. _____ Au - tumn in New York, _____

_____ it spells the thrill of first night - ing. _____
_____ it lifts you up when you're run - down. _____

Glit - ter - ing crowds and shim - mer - ing clouds in can - yons of steel, _____
Jad - ed rou - és and gay di - vor - cees who lunch at the Ritz, _____

_____ they're mak - ing me feel _____ I'm
_____ will tell you that "it's _____ di -

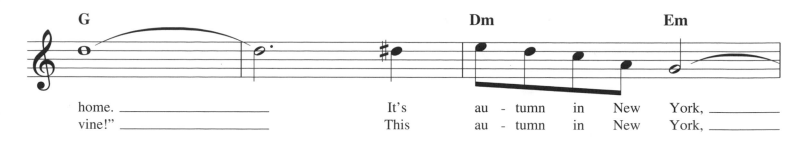

home. _____ It's au - tumn in New York, _____
vine!" _____ This au - tumn in New York, _____

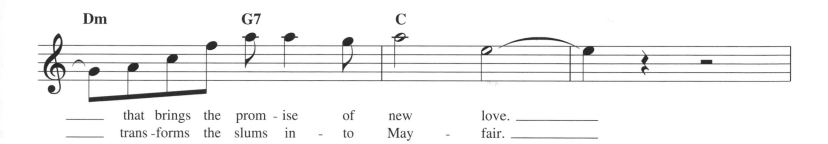

_____ that brings the prom - ise of new love. _____
_____ trans -forms the slums in - to May - fair. _____

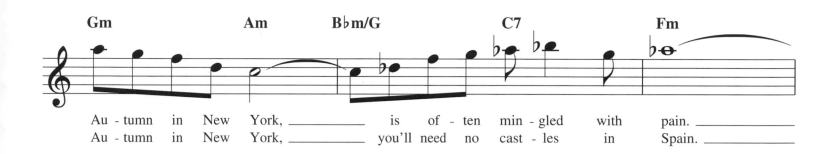

Au - tumn in New York, _____ is of - ten min - gled with pain. _____
Au - tumn in New York, _____ you'll need no cast - les in Spain. _____

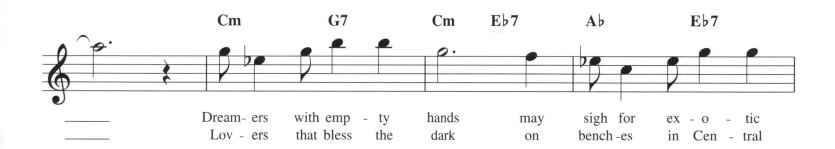

_____ Dream- ers with emp - ty hands may sigh for ex - o - tic
_____ Lov - ers that bless the dark on bench -es in Cen - tral

lands. It's au - tumn in New York, _____ it's good to live it a -
Park. Greet

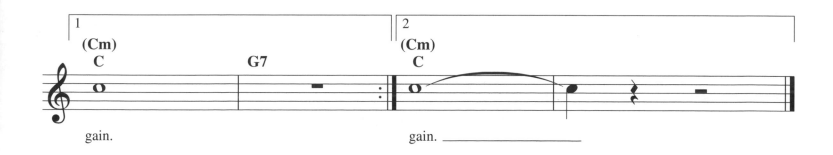

gain. _____

gain. _____

BASIN STREET BLUES

Words and Music by
SPENCER WILLIAMS

BETWEEN THE DEVIL AND THE DEEP BLUE SEA
from RHYTHMANIA

Lyric by TED KOEHLER
Music by HAROLD ARLEN

BEYOND THE BLUE HORIZON
from the Paramount Picture MONTE CARLO

Words by LEO ROBIN
Music by RICHARD A. WHITING
and W. FRANKE HARLING

BLAME IT ON MY YOUTH

Words by EDWARD HEYMAN
Music by OSCAR LEVANT

BODY AND SOUL

Words by EDWARD HEYMAN,
ROBERT SOUR and FRANK EYTON
Music by JOHN GREEN

CARAVAN
from SOPHISTICATED LADIES

Words and Music by DUKE ELLINGTON,
IRVING MILLS and JUAN TIZOL

CHANGE PARTNERS
from the RKO Radio Motion Picture CAREFREE

Words and Music by
IRVING BERLIN

Slowly

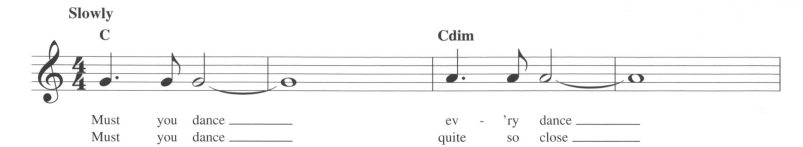

Must   you   dance _____   ev - 'ry   dance _____
Must   you   dance _____   quite   so   close _____

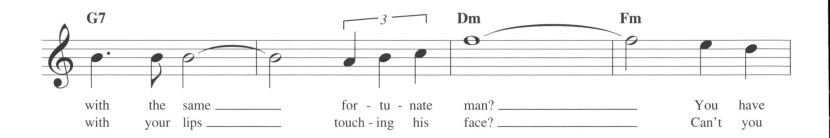

with   the   same _____   for - tu - nate   man? _____   You   have
with   your   lips _____   touch - ing   his   face? _____   Can't   you

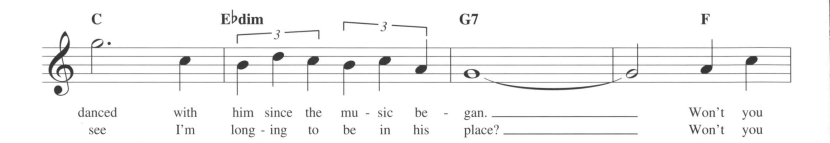

danced   with   him   since   the   mu - sic   be - gan. _____   Won't   you
see   I'm   long - ing   to   be   in   his   place? _____   Won't   you

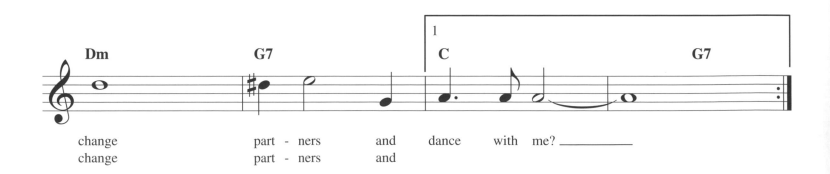

change   part - ners   and   dance   with   me? _____
change   part - ners   and

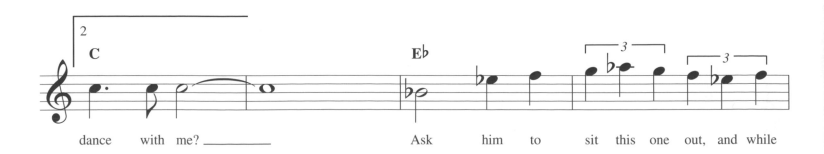

dance   with   me? _____   Ask   him   to   sit   this   one   out,   and   while

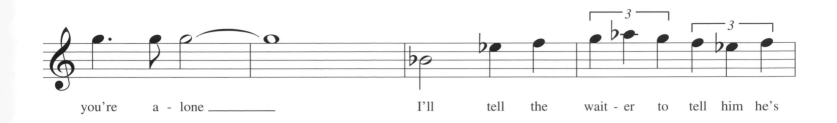

you're a - lone _____ I'll tell the wait - er to tell him he's

want - ed on the tel - e - phone. You've been locked _____

in his arms _____ ev - er since _____ heav - en knows

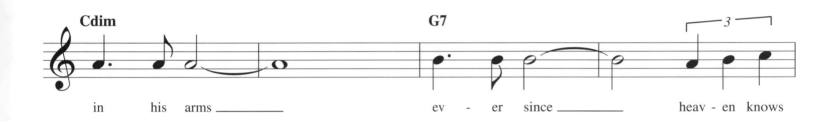

when. _____ Won't you change part - ners, and

then _____ you may nev - er want ___ to change ___

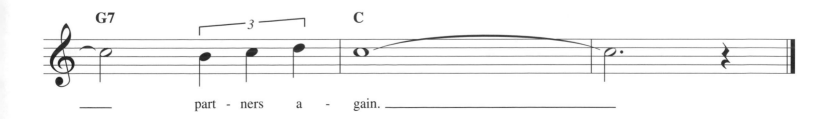

___ part - ners a - gain. _____

CHEEK TO CHEEK
from the RKO Radio Motion Picture TOP HAT

Words and Music by
IRVING BERLIN

Moderately

Heav - en, _____ I'm in heav - en. _____ And my
Heav - en _____ I'm in heav - en _____ and the

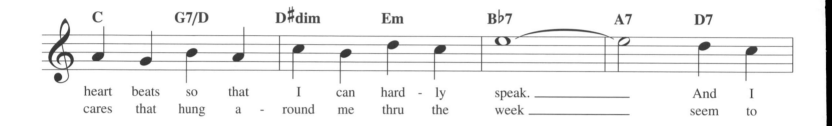

heart beats so that I can hard - ly speak. _____ And I
cares that hung a - round me thru the week _____ seem to

seem to find the hap - pi - ness I seek _____ when we're
van - ish like a gam - bler's luck - y streak _____

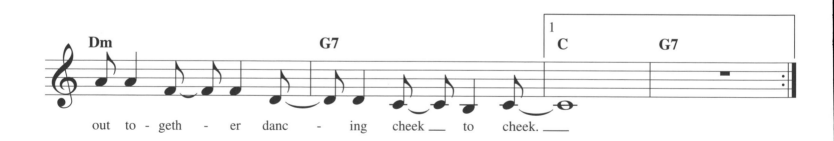

1
out to - geth - er danc - ing cheek __ to cheek. __

2
Oh, I love to climb a moun - tain, and to
love to go out fish - ing in a

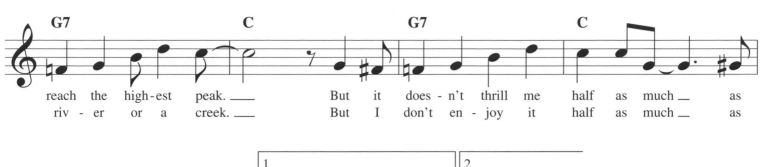

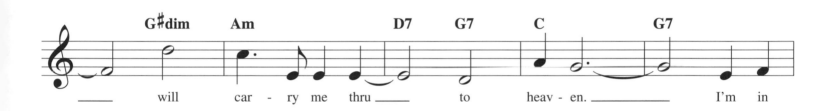

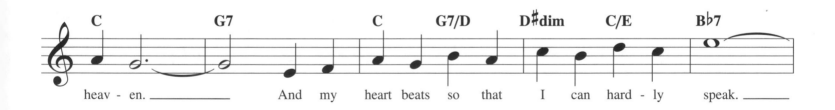

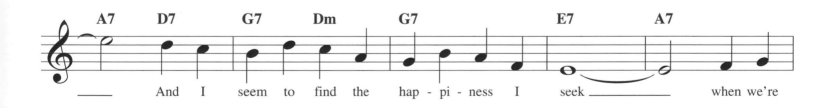

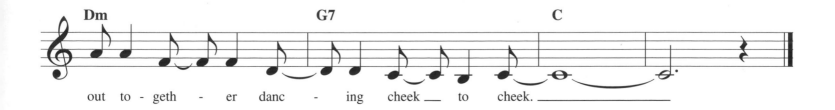

CHEROKEE
(Indian Love Song)

Words and Music by
RAY NOBLE

Moderately bright Swing

Sweet In - dian maid - en,
Child of the prai - rie,
sweet In - dian maid - en,

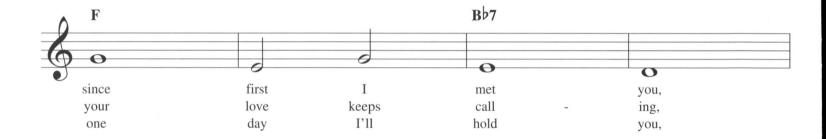

since first I met you,
your love keeps call - ing,
one day I'll hold you,

I can't for - get you,
my heart en - thrall - ing,
in my arms fold you,

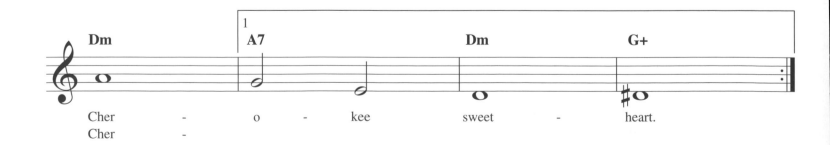

Cher - o - kee sweet - heart.
Cher -

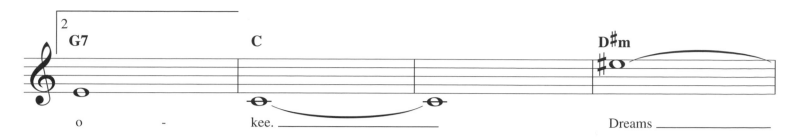

o - kee. _____ Dreams _____

_____ of sum - mer - time, _____ of

lov - er - time _____ gone by, _____

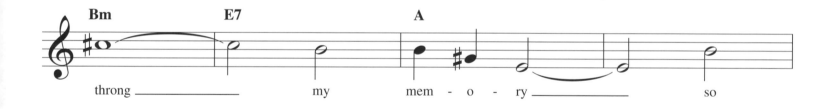

throng _____ my mem - o - ry _____ so

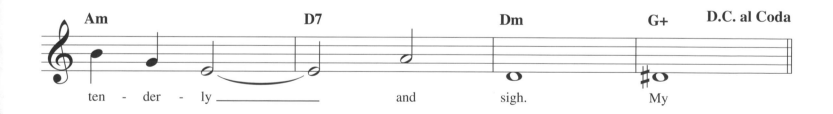

ten - der - ly _____ and sigh. My

D.C. al Coda

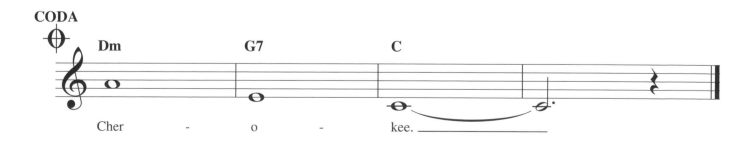

Cher - o - kee. _____

EAST OF THE SUN
(And West of the Moon)

Words and Music by
BROOKS BOWMAN

Moderately

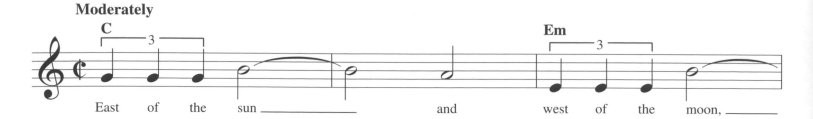

East of the sun _____ and west of the moon, _____

_____ we'll build a dream - house _____ of

love, dear. Near to the sun in the

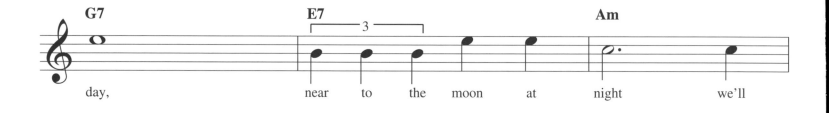

day, near to the moon at night we'll

live in a love - ly way, dear, liv - ing on love and

pale moon - light. Just you and I, _____ for -

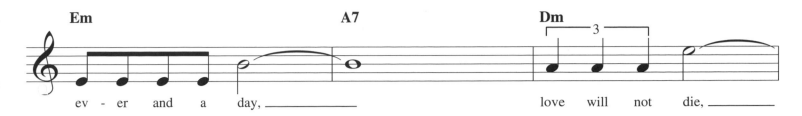

ev - er and a day, _____ love will not die, _____

_____ we'll keep it that way. _____

Up a - mong the stars we'll find a

har - mo - ny of life to a love - ly tune.

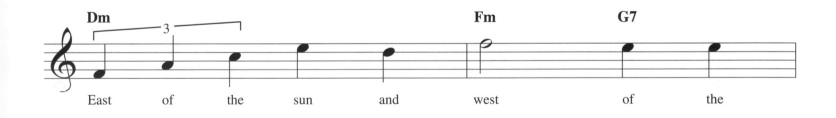

East of the sun and west of the

moon, dear, east of the sun and

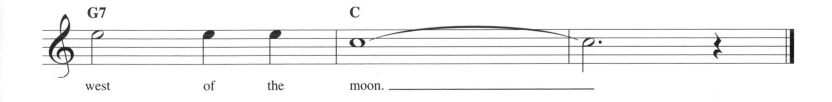

west of the moon. _____

EASTER PARADE
featured in the Motion Picture Irving Berlin's EASTER PARADE
from AS THOUSANDS CHEER

Words and Music by
IRVING BERLIN

Moderately

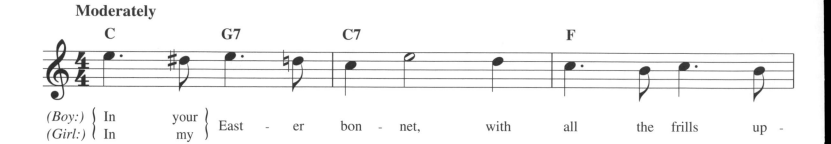

(Boy:) In your } East - er bon - net, with all the frills up -
(Girl:) In my }

on it, { you'll } be the grand - est la - dy in the
{ I'll }

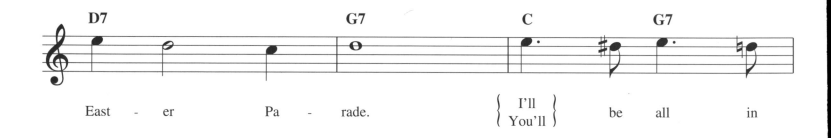

East - er Pa - rade. { I'll } be all in
{ You'll }

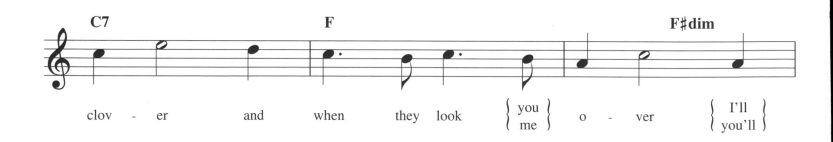

clov - er and when they look { you } o - ver { I'll }
{ me } { you'll }

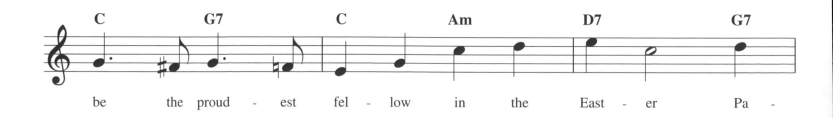

be the proud - est fel - low in the East - er Pa -

27

rade.   On the Av - e - nue, Fifth

Av - e - nue, the pho - to - graph - ers will

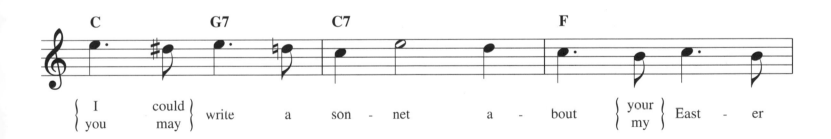

snap us. And you'll find that you're in the ro - to - gra - vure. Oh,

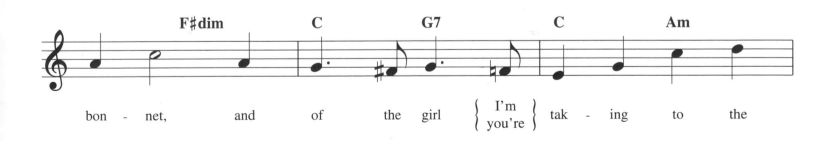

I could / you may write a son - net a - bout your / my East - er

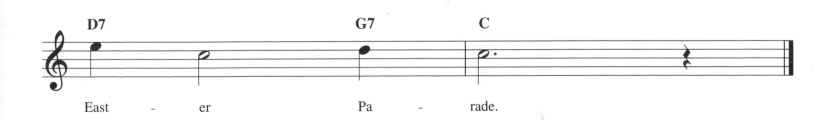

East - er Pa - rade.

EASY LIVING
Theme from the Paramount Picture EASY LIVING

Words and Music by LEO ROBIN
and RALPH RAINGER

EASY TO LOVE
(You'd Be So Easy to Love)
from BORN TO DANCE

Words and Music by
COLE PORTER

Easy Swing

You'd be so eas-y to love, so eas-y to

i-dol-ize, all oth-ers a-bove. So worth the

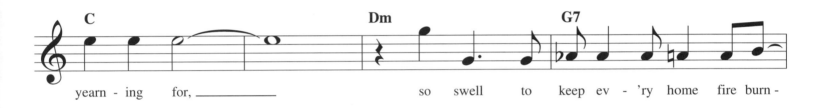

yearn-ing for, _____ so swell to keep ev-'ry home fire burn-

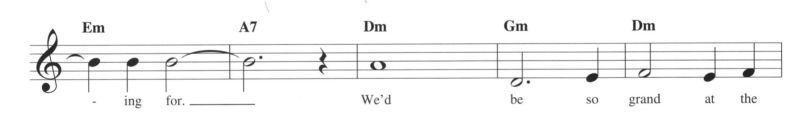

-ing for. _____ We'd be so grand at the

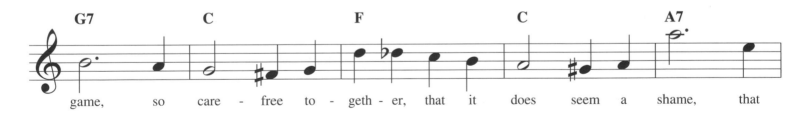

game, so care-free to-geth-er, that it does seem a shame, that

you can't see your fu-ture with me, 'cause you'd be, oh, so

eas-y to love! _____   love! _____

FALLING IN LOVE AGAIN
(Can't Help It)
from the Paramount Picture THE BLUE ANGEL

Words by SAMMY LERNER
Music by FREDERICK HOLLANDER

FALLING IN LOVE WITH LOVE
from THE BOYS FROM SYRACUSE

Words by LORENZ HART
Music by RICHARD RODGERS

A FINE ROMANCE
from SWING TIME

Words by DOROTHY FIELDS
Music by JEROME KERN

A fine ro - mance with no kiss - es, a
fine ro - mance, my good fel - low, you

fine ro - mance, my friend, this is! We
take ro - mance, I'll take jel - lo! You're

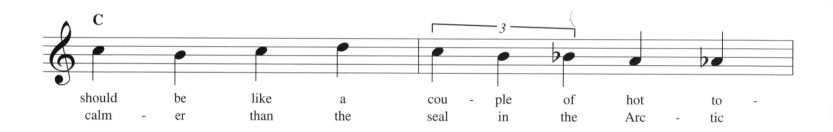

should be like a cou - ple of hot to -
calm - er than the seal in the Arc - tic

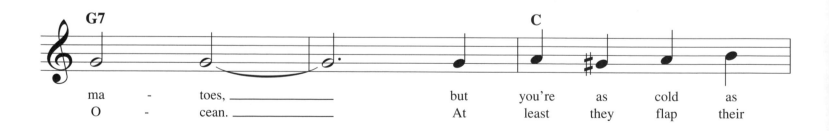

ma - toes, _____ but you're as cold as
O - cean. _____ At least they flap their

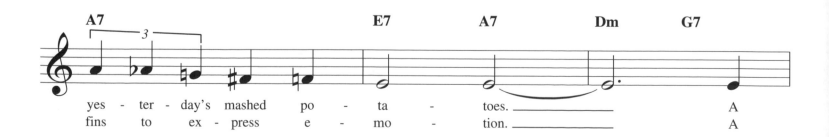

yes - ter - day's mashed po - ta - toes. _____ A
fins to ex - press e - mo - tion. _____ A

fine ro - mance, you won't nes - tle. A
fine ro - mance with no quar - rels, with

fine ro - mance, you won't wres - tle! I
no in - sults, and all mor - als! I've

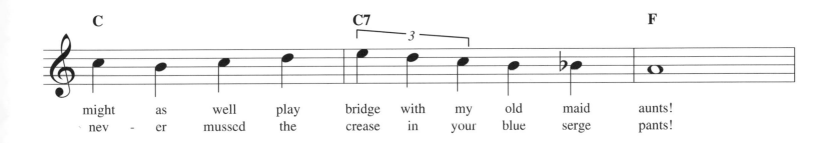

might as well play bridge with my old maid aunts!
nev - er mussed the crease in your blue serge pants!

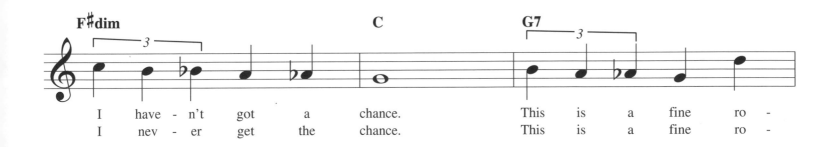

I have - n't got a chance. This is a fine ro -
I nev - er get the chance. This is a fine ro -

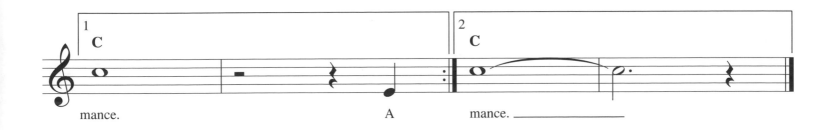

mance. A mance. _____

THE FOLKS WHO LIVE ON THE HILL
from HIGH, WIDE AND HANDSOME

Lyric by OSCAR HAMMERSTEIN II
Music by JEROME KERN

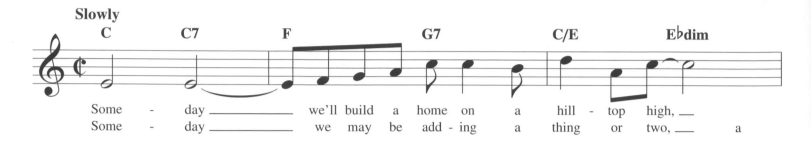

Some - day _____ we'll build a home on a hill - top high, _____
Some - day _____ we may be add - ing a thing or two, _____ a

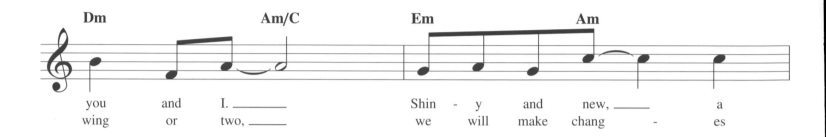

you and I. _____ Shin - y and new, _____ a
wing or two, _____ we will make chang - es

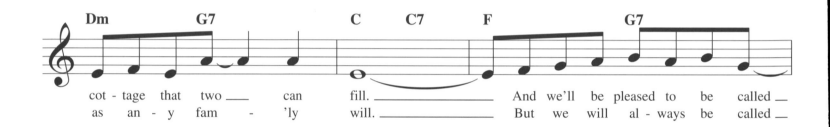

cot - tage that two _____ can fill. _____ And we'll be pleased to be called _____
as an - y fam - 'ly will. _____ But we will al - ways be called _____

_____ "The Folks Who Live On The Hill." _____
_____ "The Folks Who Live On The Hill." _____

_____ Our _____ ve - ran - da will com - mand a view of mead - ows

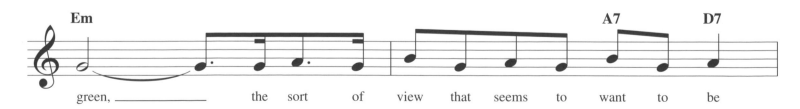

green, _____ the sort of view that seems to want to be

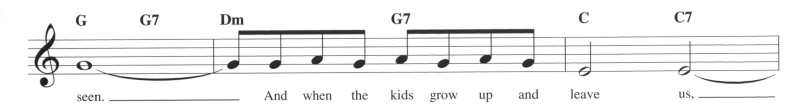

seen. _____ And when the kids grow up and leave us, _____

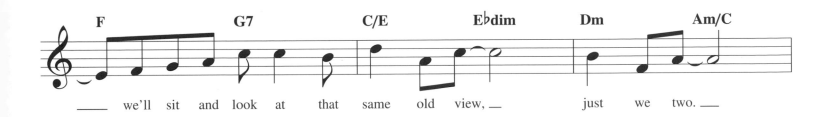

____ we'll sit and look at that same old view, ___ just we two. ___

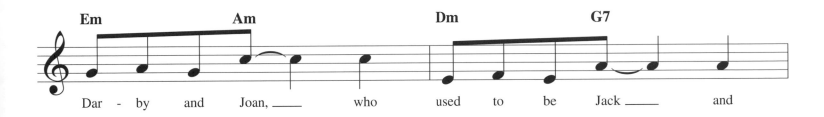

Dar - by and Joan, ___ who used to be Jack ____ and

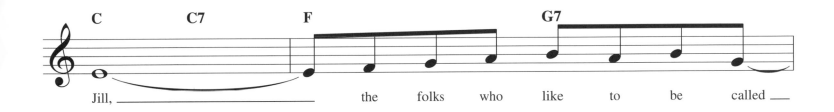

Jill, _____ the folks who like to be called ___

_____ what they have al - ways been called, ___

_____ "The Folks Who Live On The Hill." ___

FOR ALL WE KNOW

Words by SAM M. LEWIS
Music by J. FRED COOTS

GEORGIA ON MY MIND

Words by STUART GORRELL
Music by HOAGY CARMICHAEL

Slowly

GLAD TO BE UNHAPPY
from ON YOUR TOES

Words by LORENZ HART
Music by RICHARD RODGERS

Reflectively

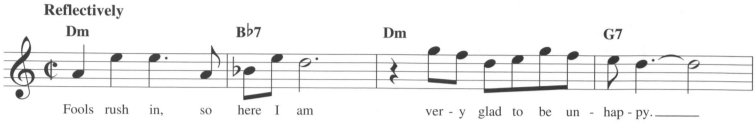

Fools rush in, so here I am ver-y glad to be un-hap-py. _____

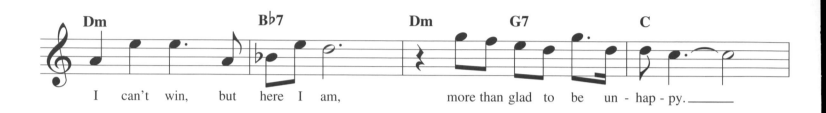

I can't win, but here I am, more than glad to be un-hap-py. _____

Un-re-quit-ed love's a bore, and I've got it pret-ty bad.

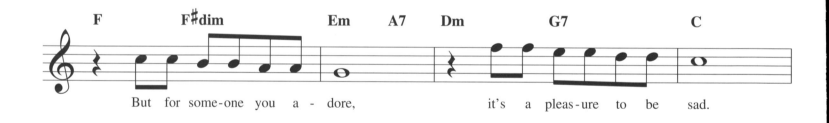

But for some-one you a-dore, it's a pleas-ure to be sad.

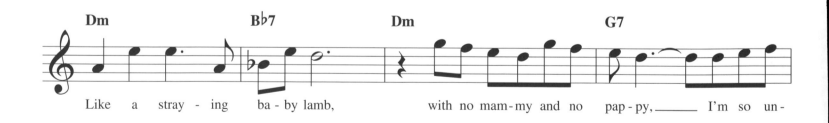

Like a stray-ing ba-by lamb, with no mam-my and no pap-py, _____ I'm so un-

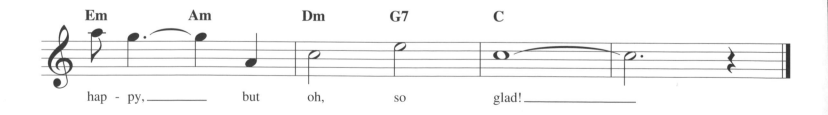

hap-py, _____ but oh, so glad! _____

THE GLORY OF LOVE
from GUESS WHO'S COMING TO DINNER

Words and Music by
BILLY HILL

GOODBYE

Words and Music by
GORDON JENKINS

Slowly

I'll nev - er for - get you, _____ I'll

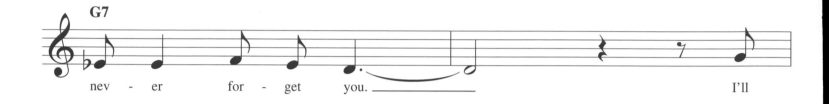

nev - er for - get you. _____ I'll

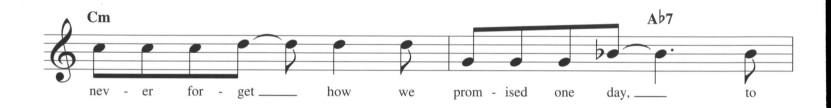

nev - er for - get _____ how we prom - ised one day, _____ to

love one an - oth - er for - ev - er that way. _____ We

said we'd nev - er say _____ good - bye.

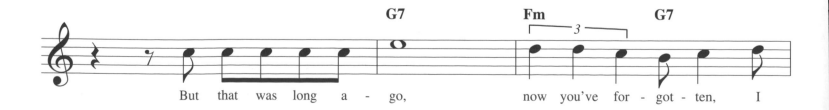

But that was long a - go, now you've for - got - ten, I

know. No use to won - der why,

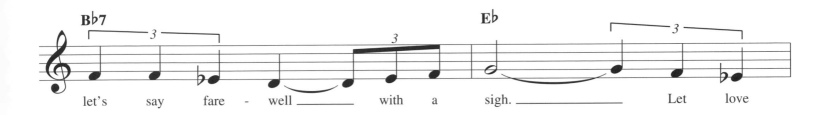

let's say fare - well _____ with a sigh. _____ Let love

die. But we'll go on liv - ing _____ our

own way of liv - ing, _____ so

you take the high ____ road and I'll take the low. ____ It's

time that we part - ed, it's much bet - ter so. _____ But

kiss me as you go, _____ good - bye. _____

HAVE YOU EVER BEEN LONELY?
(Have You Ever Been Blue?)

Words by GEORGE BROWN
Music by PETER DeROSE

HEART AND SOUL
from the Paramount Short Subject A SONG IS BORN

Words by FRANK LOESSER
Music by HOAGY CARMICHAEL

Heart and soul, I fell in love with you heart and soul, the way a fool would do,
Heart and soul, I begged to be a-dored, lost con-trol and tum-bled o-ver-board

mad-ly, be-cause you held me tight ____ and stole a kiss in the night. __
glad-ly, the mag-ic night we kissed ____ there in the

moon-mist. Oh! But your lips were thrill-ing, much too

thrill-ing. Nev-er be-fore were mine so strange-ly

will-ing. But now I see what one em-brace can do. Look at me,

it's got me lov-ing you mad-ly, that lit-tle kiss you stole

held all my heart and soul. ____

HEARTACHES

Words by JOHN KLENNER
Music by AL HOFFMAN

Moderately

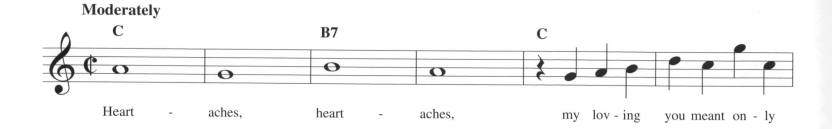

Heart - aches, heart - aches, my lov - ing you meant on - ly

heart - aches. Your kiss was such a sa - cred thing to me, _____

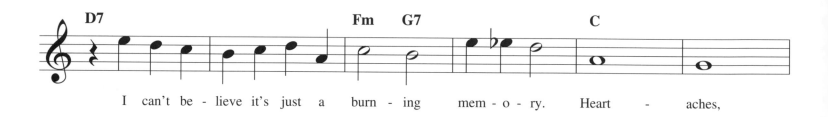

I can't be - lieve it's just a burn - ing mem - o - ry. Heart - aches,

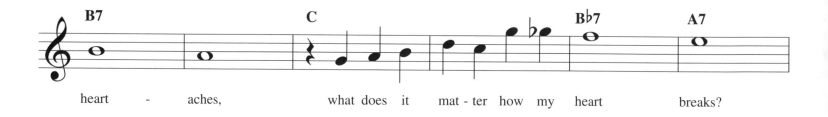

heart - aches, what does it mat - ter how my heart breaks?

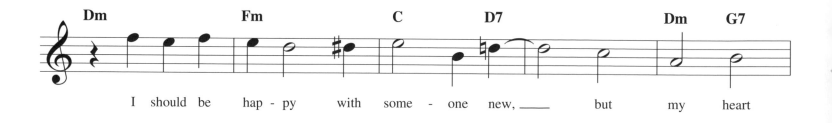

I should be hap - py with some - one new, _____ but my heart

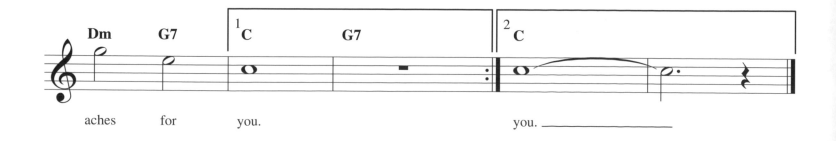

aches for you. you. _____

HONEYSUCKLE ROSE
from AIN'T MISBEHAVIN'

Words by ANDY RAZAF
Music by THOMAS "FATS" WALLER

Moderately, with a lilt

Ev - 'ry hon - ey bee fills with jeal - ous - y
When you're pass - in' by flow - ers droop and sigh,

when they see you out with me. I don't blame 'em,
and I know the rea - son why. You're much sweet - er,

good - ness knows. _____ Hon - ey - suck - le Rose. _____

Don't buy sug - ar. You just have to

touch my cup. You're my sug - ar.

It's sweet when you stir it up. _____ When I'm tak - in' sips

from your tast - y lips, seems the hon - ey fair - ly drips. You're con - fec - tion,

good - ness knows. _____ Hon - ey - suck - le Rose. _____

HOW DEEP IS THE OCEAN
(How High Is the Sky)

Words and Music by
IRVING BERLIN

How much do I love you? I'll tell you no lie.

How deep is the o - cean, how high is the sky?

How man - y times a day __ do I think of you? _____

How man - y ros - es are sprin - kled with dew? ___ How far would I

trav - el to be where you are? How far is the jour - ney

from here to a star? And if I ev - er lost you, how much would I

cry? How deep is the o - cean, how high is the sky?

I DIDN'T KNOW WHAT TIME IT WAS
from TOO MANY GIRLS

Words by LORENZ HART
Music by RICHARD RODGERS

Slowly and tenderly

I CAN'T GET STARTED WITH YOU
from ZIEGFELD FOLLIES

Words by IRA GERSHWIN
Music by VERNON DUKE

Moderately

I've flown a - round the world __ in a plane; _____ I've set - tled
hun - dred yards __ in ten flat; _____ the Prince of

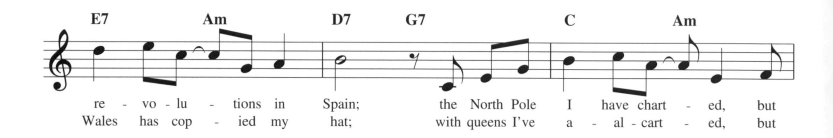

re - vo - lu - tions in Spain; the North Pole I have chart - ed, but
Wales has cop - ied my hat; with queens I've a - al - cart - ed, but

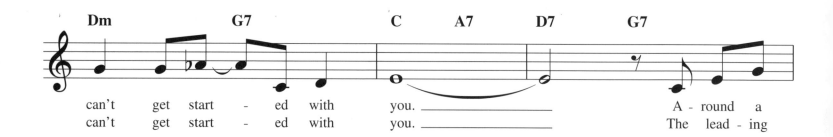

can't get start - ed with you. _____ A - round a
can't get start - ed with you. _____ The lead - ing

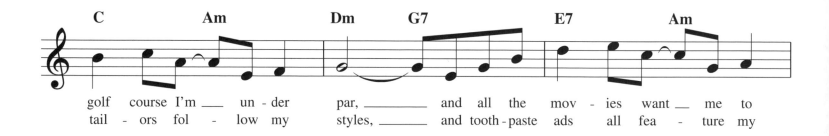

golf course I'm __ un - der par, _____ and all the mov - ies want __ me to
tail - ors fol - low my styles, _____ and tooth - paste ads all fea - ture my

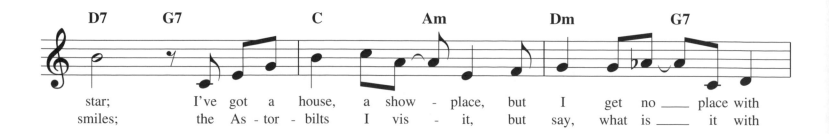

star; I've got a house, a show - place, but I get no __ place with
smiles; the As - tor - bilts I vis - it, but say, what is __ it with

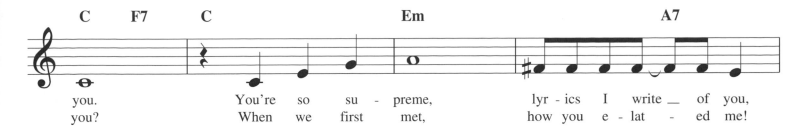

you.
you?

You're so su - preme,
When we first met,

lyr - ics I write __ of you,
how you e - lat - ed me!

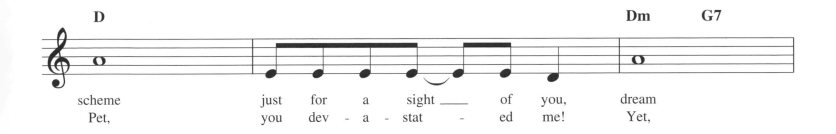

scheme
Pet,

just for a sight ___ of you, dream
you dev - a - stat - ed me! Yet,

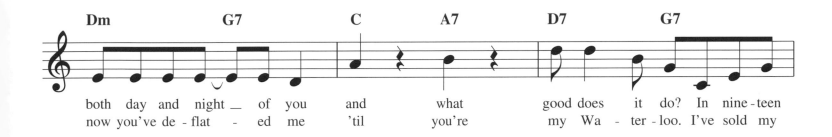

both day and night __ of you and
now you've de - flat - ed me 'til

what
you're

good does it do? In nine - teen
my Wa - ter - loo. I've sold my

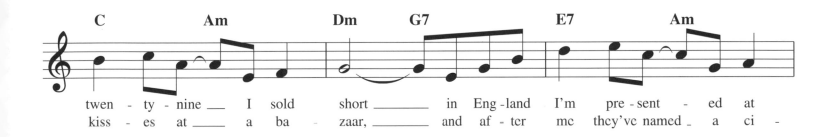

twen - ty - nine __ I sold
kiss - es at ___ a ba

short _____ in Eng - land I'm pre - sent - ed at
zaar, _____ and af - ter me they've named _ a ci -

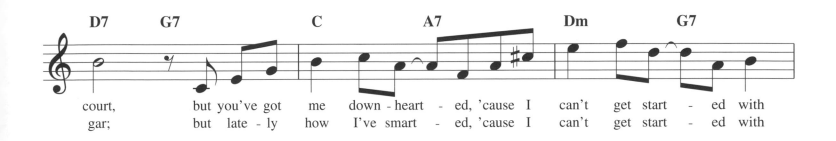

court,
gar;

but you've got me down - heart - ed, 'cause I
but late - ly how I've smart - ed, 'cause I

can't get start - ed with
can't get start - ed with

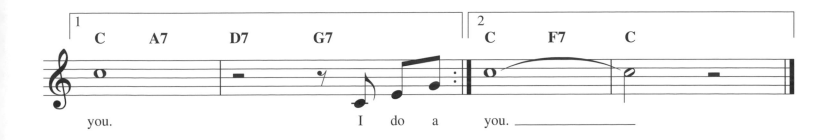

you.

I do a

you. _____

I DON'T KNOW WHY
(I Just Do)

Lyric by ROY TURK
Music by FRED E. AHLERT

Slowly, with feeling

I don't know why ____ I love you like I do. ____

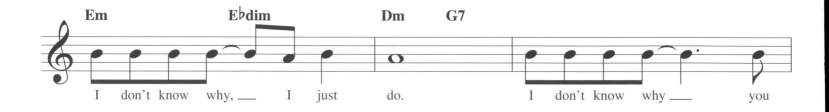

I don't know why, ____ I just do. I don't know why ____ you

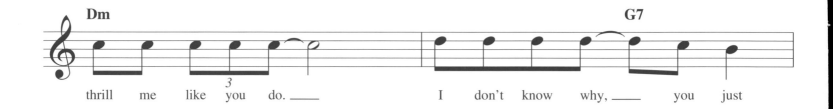

thrill me like you do. ____ I don't know why, ____ you just

do. You nev-er seem to want my ro-manc-ing. The

on-ly time you hold me is when we're danc-ing.

I don't know why ____ I love you like I do. ____

I don't know why, ____ I just do.

I DON'T STAND A GHOST OF A CHANCE

Words by BING CROSBY and NED WASHINGTON
Music by VICTOR YOUNG

I WANNA BE LOVED

Words by BILLY ROSE and EDWARD HEYMAN
Music by JOHN GREEN

Moderately

I wan-na be loved _____ with in-spi-ra-tion. _____ I wan-na be
loved _____ with in-spi-ra-tion. _____ I wan-na be

loved start-ing to-night. In-stead of mere-ly hold-ing con-ver-
loved start-ing to-night. In-stead of mere-ly hold-ing con-ver-

sa - tion, _____ hold me tight! I wan-na be
sa - tion, _____ hold me tight! I wan-na be

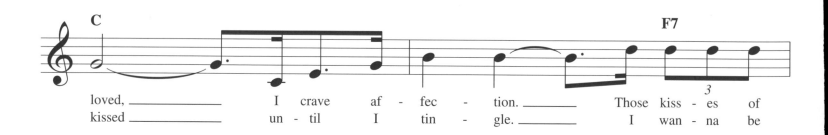

loved, _____ I crave af-fec-tion. _____ Those kiss-es of
kissed _____ un-til I tin-gle. _____ I wan-na be

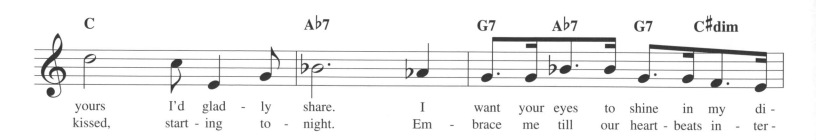

yours I'd glad-ly share. I want your eyes to shine in my di-
kissed, start-ing to-night. Em-brace me till our heart-beats in-ter-

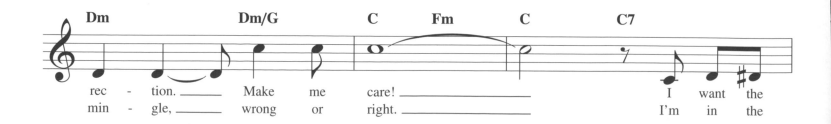

rec - tion. _____ Make me care! _____ I want the
min - gle, _____ wrong or right. _____ I'm in the

kind of ro - mance ___ that should be strong and e - qual - ly as
mood to a - dore. ___ I'm read - y for that well - known tur - tle -

ten - der. ___ I on - ly ask for the chance ___ to know the
dov - ing. ___ I'm in no mood to re - sist, ___ and I in -

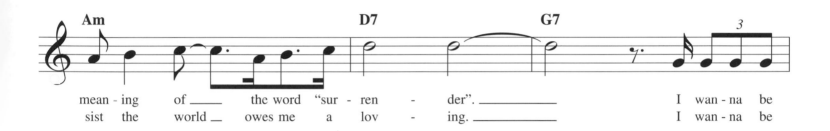

mean - ing of ___ the word "sur - ren - der". ___ I wan - na be
sist the world ___ owes me a lov - ing. ___ I wan - na be

thrilled ___ by on - ly you, dear. ___ I wan - na be thrilled by your ca -
thrilled ___ to des - per - a - tion, ___ I wan - na be thrilled start - ing to -

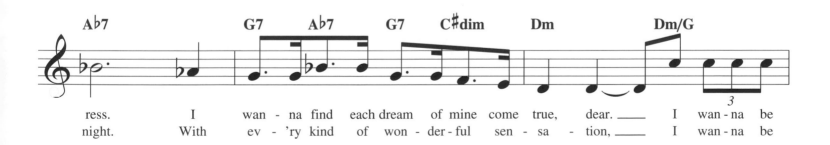

ress. I wan - na find each dream of mine come true, dear. ___ I wan - na be
night. With ev - 'ry kind of won - der - ful sen - sa - tion, ___ I wan - na be

loved!   I wan - na be   loved! ___

I WON'T DANCE
from ROBERTA

Words and Music by JIMMY McHUGH,
DOROTHY FIELDS, JEROME KERN,
OSCAR HAMMERSTEIN II and OTTO HARBACH

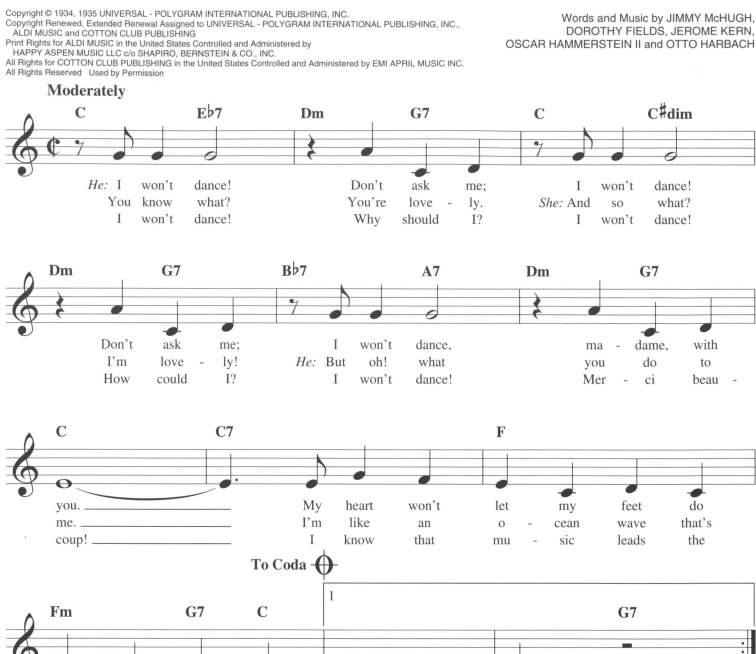

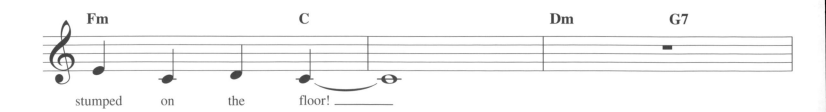

She: When you dance you're charm - ing and you're gen - tle! _____

'Spec - ially when you do the "Con - ti -

nen - tal." _____ *He:* But this feel - ing is - n't pure - ly

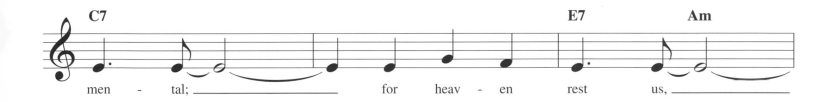

men - tal; _____ for heav - en rest us, _____

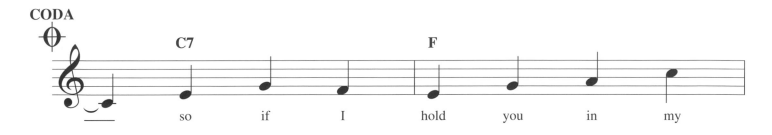

_____ I'm not as - bes - tos. _____ And that's why

_____ so if I hold you in my

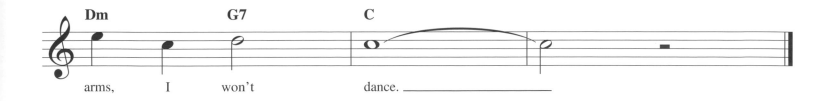

arms, I won't dance. _____

I'LL BE SEEING YOU

from RIGHT THIS WAY

Lyric by IRVING KAHAL
Music by SAMMY FAIN

Slowly

I'LL NEVER SMILE AGAIN

Words and Music by
RUTH LOWE

I'LL TAKE ROMANCE

Lyrics by OSCAR HAMMERSTEIN II
Music by BEN OAKLAND

Moderate Waltz

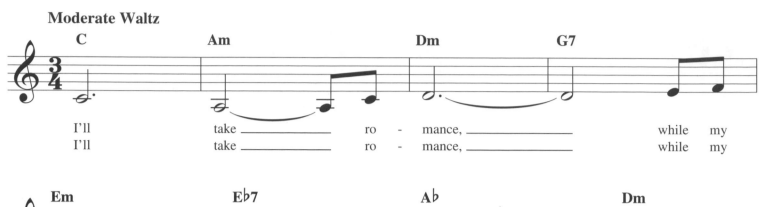

I'll take ———— ro - mance, ———— while my
I'll take ———— ro - mance, ———— while my

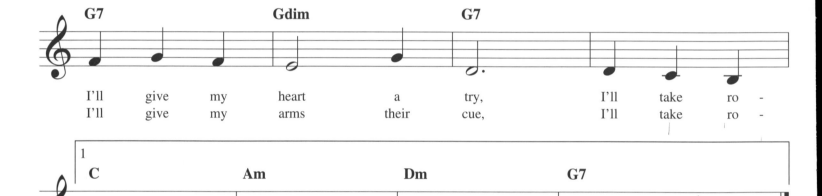

heart is young and ea - ger to fly.
arms are strong and ea - ger for you.

I'll give my heart a try, I'll take ro -
I'll give my arms their cue, I'll take ro -

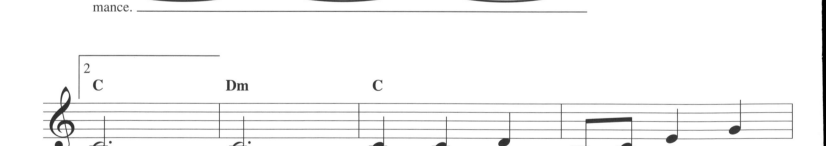

mance. ————

mance. ———— So, my lov - er, when you

want me, call me

I'M PUTTING ALL MY EGGS IN ONE BASKET

from the Motion Picture FOLLOW THE FLEET

Words and Music by
IRVING BERLIN

Lord help me if ____ my ba - by don't come through. ____

____ I've got a great ____ big a - mount ____ saved up in

my love ac - count, ____ hon - ey, and I've de - cid - ed

love di - vid - ed in two won't do. So

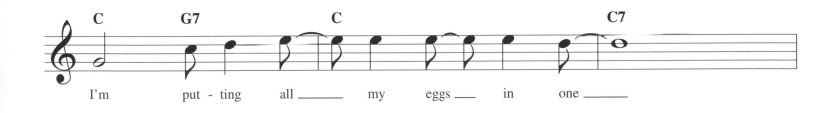

I'm put - ting all ____ my eggs ____ in one ____

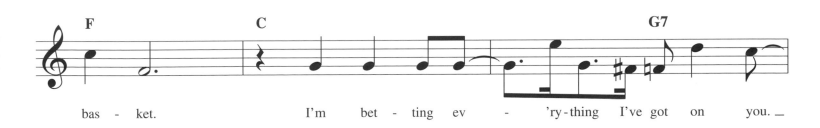

bas - ket. I'm bet - ting ev - 'ry-thing I've got on you. __

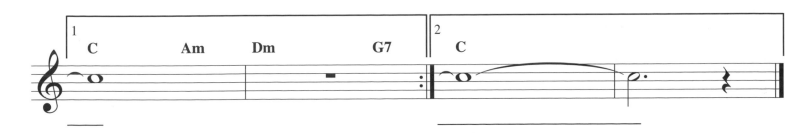

I'VE GOT MY LOVE TO KEEP ME WARM
from the 20th Century Fox Motion Picture ON THE AVENUE

Words and Music by
IRVING BERLIN

Bright jump tempo

The snow is snow-ing, the wind is
can't re-mem-ber a worse De-

blow-ing, but I can weath-er the storm.
cem-ber; just watch those i-ci-cles form.

What do I care how
What do I care if

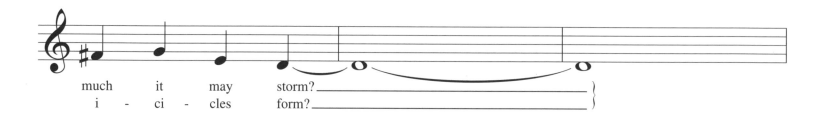

much it may storm?
i-ci-cles form?

I've got my love to keep me warm.

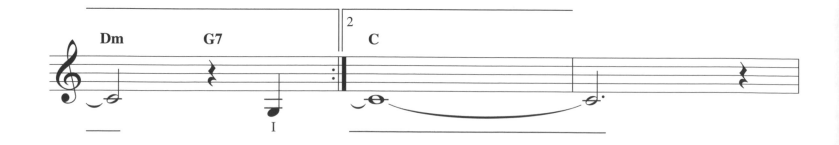

63

I'VE GOT THE WORLD ON A STRING

Lyric by TED KOEHLER
Music by HAROLD ARLEN

Easy Swing

I've got the world on a string, _ sit-tin' on a rain-bow, got the string a-round my fin - ger.
song that I sing, _ I can make the rain go, an-y-time I move my fin - ger.

What a world, what a _____ life, _ I'm in love!   I've got a
Luck - y me, can't you _ see, _ I'm in

love? _____ Life is a beau - ti - ful thing _____

as long as I hold the string, ___   I'd be a sil - ly so and

so   if I should ev - er let go. _____ I've got the

world on a string, _ sit - tin' on a rain-bow, got the string a-round my fin -

- ger.   What a world, what a _____ life, _ I'm in love. _____

IT'S EASY TO REMEMBER
from the Paramount Picture MISSISSIPPI

Words by LORENZ HART
Music by RICHARD RODGERS

Slowly, expressively

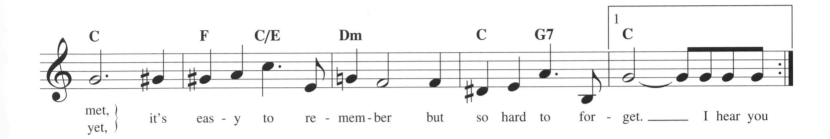

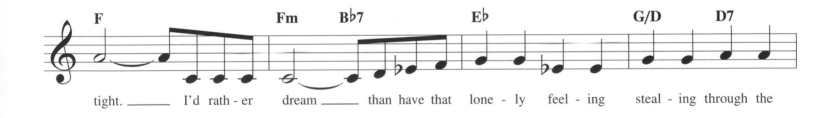

I'VE GOT YOU UNDER MY SKIN
from BORN TO DANCE

Words and Music by
COLE PORTER

Moderately

I've got you _____ un-der my skin. _____ I've

got you _____ deep in the heart of me, _____ so

deep in my heart, _____ you're real-ly a part of me. _____ I've

got you _____ un-der my skin. _____ I

tried so _____ not to give in. _____ I

said to my-self, "This af-fair nev-er will go so well." _____ But

why should I try to re-sist when, dar-ling, I know so well _____ I've

IN THE MOOD

By JOE GARLAND

Moderate Swing

IN THE STILL OF THE NIGHT
from ROSALIE

Words and Music by
COLE PORTER

Moderately, mysteriously

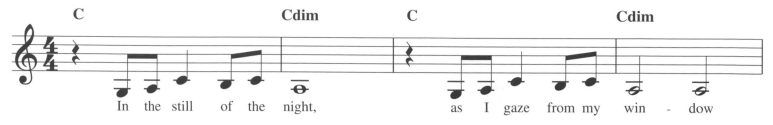

In the still of the night, as I gaze from my win - dow

at the moon in its flight my thoughts all stray to you. _____

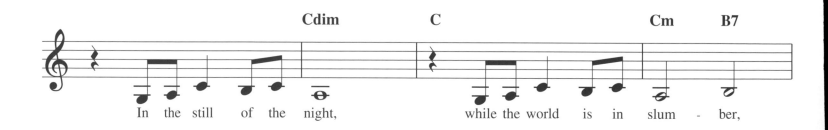

In the still of the night, while the world is in slum - ber,

oh, the times with - out num - ber, dar - ling, when I say to you: _____

"Do you love me as I love you?"

Are you my life - to - be, my dream come true.

Or will this dream of mine fade out of sight like the

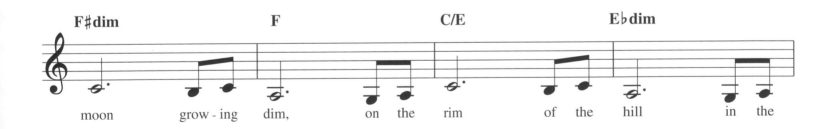

moon grow - ing dim, on the rim of the hill in the

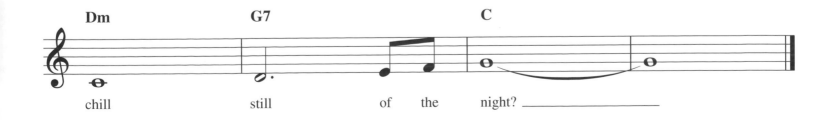

chill still of the night? _____

ISN'T IT ROMANTIC?
from the Paramount Picture LOVE ME TONIGHT

Words by LORENZ HART
Music by RICHARD RODGERS

Steadily, not too fast

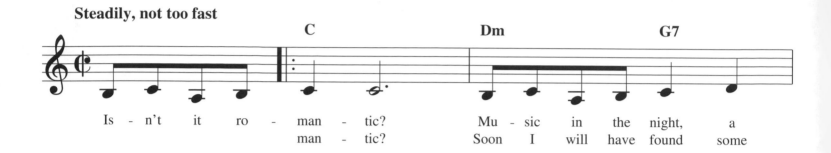

Is - n't it ro - man - tic? Mu - sic in the night, a
man - tic? Soon I will have found some

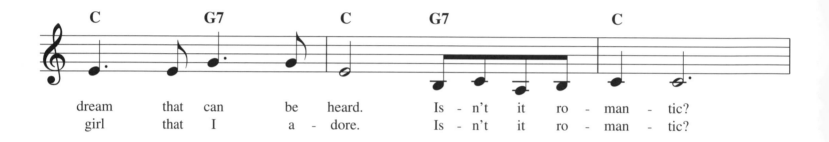

dream that can be heard. Is - n't it ro - man - tic?
girl that I a - dore. Is - n't it ro - man - tic?

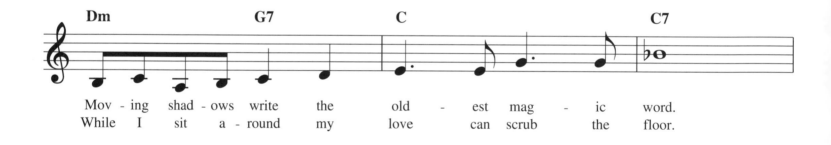

Mov - ing shad - ows write the old - est mag - ic word.
While I sit a - round my love can scrub the floor.

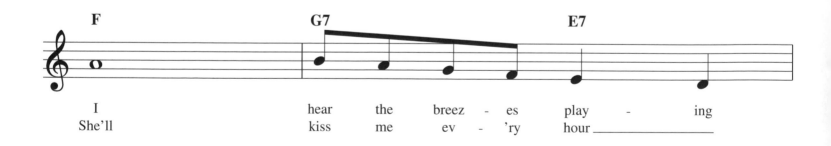

I hear the breez - es play - ing
She'll kiss me ev - 'ry hour

in the trees a - bove.
or she'll get the sack.

IT'S DE-LOVELY
from RED, HOT AND BLUE!

Words and Music by
COLE PORTER

The night is young, ___ the skies are clear ___ and

if you want ___ to go walk - ing, dear, ___ it's de -

light - ful, ___ it's de - li - cious, ___ it's de - love - ly. ___

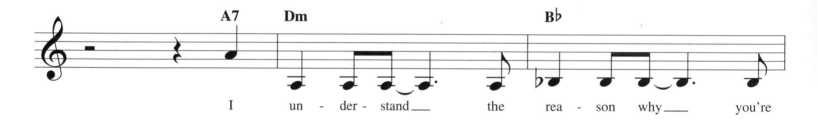

I un - der - stand ___ the rea - son why ___ you're

sen - ti - men - tal, 'cause so am I, ___ it's de - light - ful, ___ it's de -

li - cious, ___ it's de - love - ly. ___ You can

tell at a glance ___ what a swell night ___ this

IT'S ONLY A PAPER MOON

Lyric by BILLY ROSE and E.Y. "YIP" HARBURG
Music by HAROLD ARLEN

Moderately

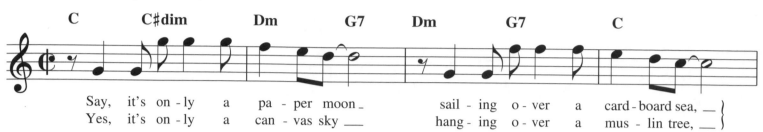

Say, it's on-ly a pa-per moon_ sail-ing o-ver a card-board sea, _
Yes, it's on-ly a can-vas sky _ hang-ing o-ver a mus-lin tree, _

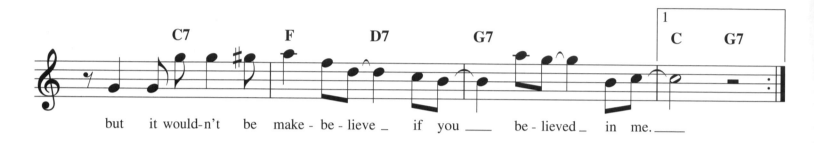

but it would-n't be make-be-lieve _ if you ____ be-lieved _ in me. ____

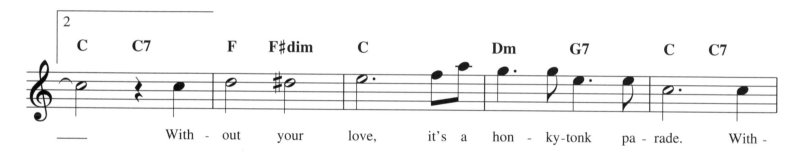

____ With-out your love, it's a hon-ky-tonk pa-rade. With-

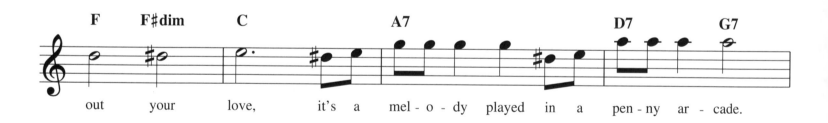

out your love, it's a mel-o-dy played in a pen-ny ar-cade.

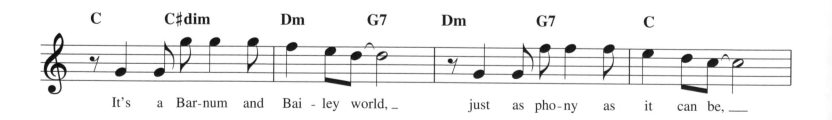

It's a Bar-num and Bai-ley world, _ just as pho-ny as it can be, ___

but it would-n't be make-be-lieve _ if you ___ be-lieved _ in me. ___

JUNE IN JANUARY
from the Paramount Picture HERE IS MY HEART

Words and Music by LEO ROBIN
and RALPH RAINGER

JUST ONE MORE CHANCE

Words by SAM COSLOW
Music by ARTHUR JOHNSTON

THE LADY IS A TRAMP
from BABES IN ARMS

Words by LORENZ HART
Music by RICHARD RODGERS

THE LADY'S IN LOVE WITH YOU
from the Paramount Picture SOME LIKE IT HOT

Words by FRANK LOESSER
Music by BURTON LANE

Moderately, rhythmically

If there's a gleam in her eye ____ each time she straight-ens your tie, ___
dress for a date ____ with-out that wait-ing you hate, ___

____ you'll know the la-dy's in love ____ with you. If she can
____ it means the la-dy's in love ____ with

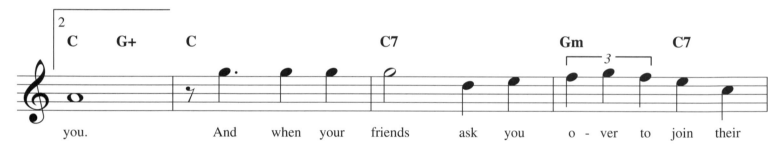

you. And when your friends ask you o-ver to join their

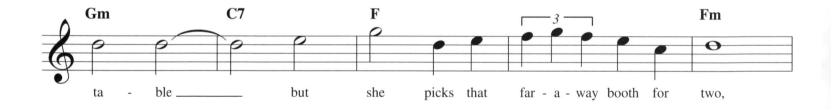

ta - ble _____ but she picks that far-a-way booth for two,

well, sir, here's just how it stands, ___ you've got ro-mance on your hands __

____ be-cause the la-dy's in love ____ with you. _____

LAZY RIVER

from THE BEST YEARS OF OUR LIVES

Words and Music by HOAGY CARMICHAEL
and SIDNEY ARODIN

Up a la-zy riv-er by the old mill-run, that la-zy, la-zy riv-er in the

noon-day sun, lin-ger in the shade of a kind old tree;

throw a-way your trou-bles, dream a dream with me. __ Up a la-zy riv-er where the

rob-in's song a-wakes a bright new morn-ing, we can loaf a-long.

Blue skies up a-bove, ev-'ry-one's in love, up a la-zy riv-er, how

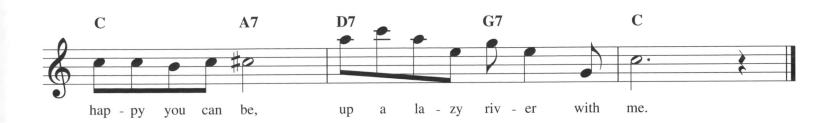

hap-py you can be, up a la-zy riv-er with me.

LET'S FACE THE MUSIC AND DANCE
from the Motion Picture FOLLOW THE FLEET

Words and Music by
IRVING BERLIN

Moderately

There may be trou - ble a - head. _____

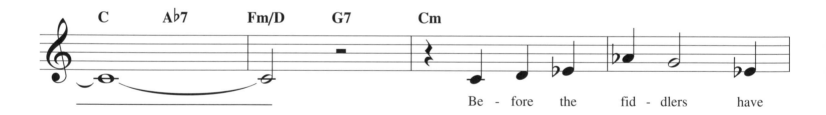

But while there's moon - light and mu - sic and love and ro -

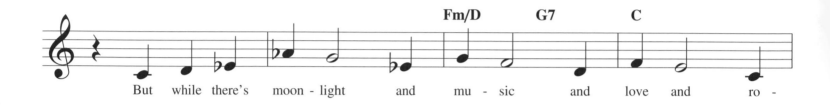

mance, _____ let's face the mu - sic and dance. _

Be - fore the fid - dlers have

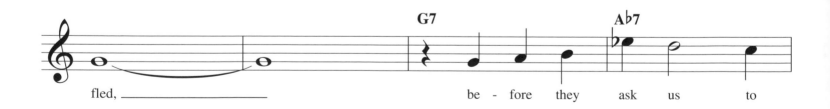

fled, _____ be - fore they ask us to

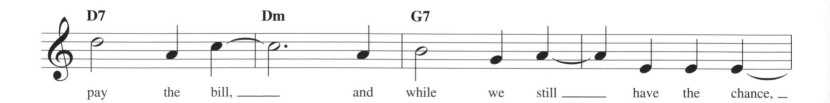

pay the bill, ___ and while we still ___ have the chance, _

LITTLE GIRL BLUE
from JUMBO

Words by LORENZ HART
Music by RICHARD RODGERS

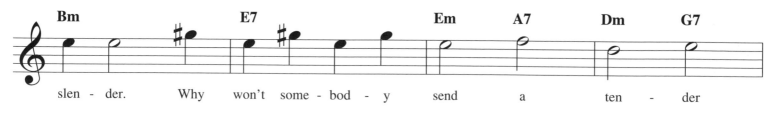

LOVE IS JUST AROUND THE CORNER
from the Paramount Picture HERE IS MY HEART

Words and Music by LEO ROBIN
and LEWIS E. GENSLER

LOVER
from the Paramount Picture LOVE ME TONIGHT

Lyrics by LORENZ HART
Music by RICHARD RODGERS

Lov - er, _____ when I'm near you _____ and I

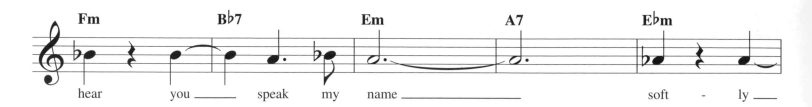

hear you _____ speak my name _____ soft - ly _____

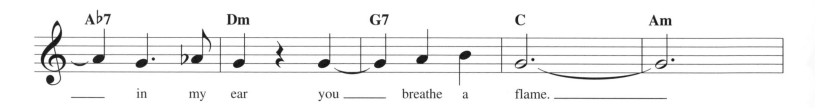

_____ in my ear you _____ breathe a flame. _____

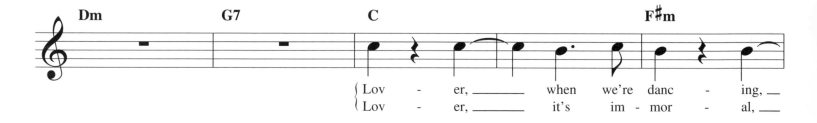

Lov - er, _____ when we're danc - ing, __
Lov - er, _____ it's im - mor - al, __

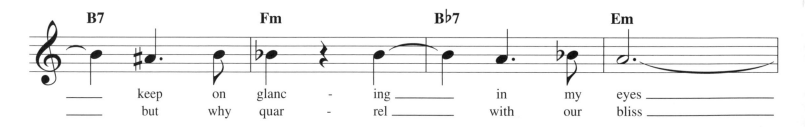

_____ keep on glanc - ing _____ in my eyes _____
_____ but why quar - rel _____ with our bliss _____

_____ till love's _____ own en - tranc - ing _____
_____ when two _____ lips of cor - al _____

_____ mu - sic dies. _____
_____ want to kiss? _____

MEMORIES OF YOU
from THE BENNY GOODMAN STORY

Lyric by ANDY RAZAF
Music by EUBIE BLAKE

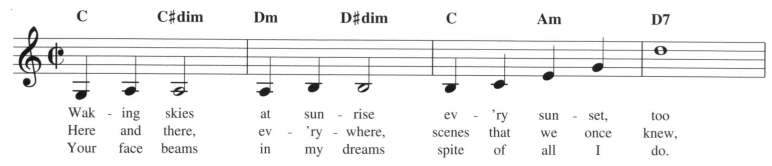

Wak - ing skies at sun - rise ev - 'ry sun - set, too
Here and there, ev - 'ry - where, scenes that we once knew,
Your face beams in my dreams spite of all I do.

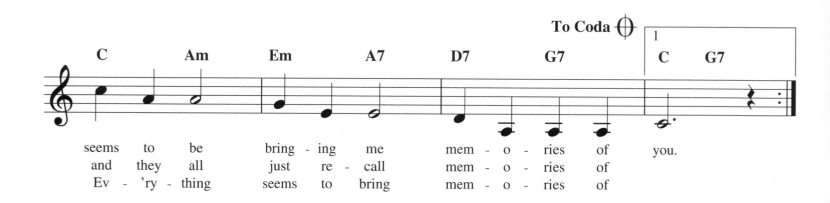

seems to be bring - ing me mem - o - ries of you.
and they all just re - call mem - o - ries of
Ev - 'ry - thing seems to bring mem - o - ries of

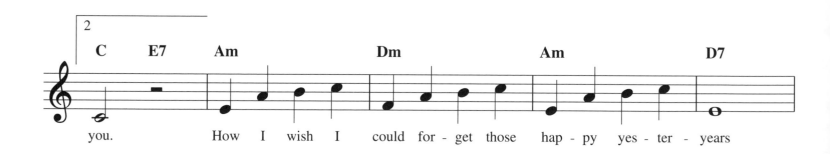

you. How I wish I could for - get those hap - py yes - ter - years

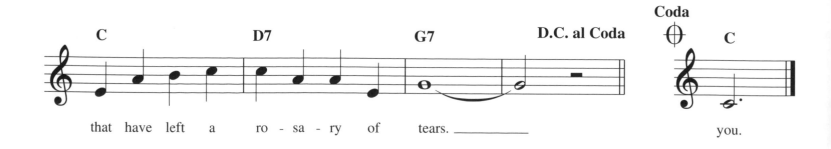

that have left a ro - sa - ry of tears. _____

you.

MOOD INDIGO
from SOPHISTICATED LADIES

Words and Music by DUKE ELLINGTON,
IRVING MILLS and ALBANY BIGARD

MOONGLOW

Words and Music by WILL HUDSON,
EDDIE DE LANGE and IRVING MILLS

MY BABY JUST CARES FOR ME
from WHOOPEE!

Lyrics by GUS KAHN
Music by WALTER DONALDSON

MY FUNNY VALENTINE
from BABES IN ARMS

Words by LORENZ HART
Music by RICHARD RODGERS

Slowly

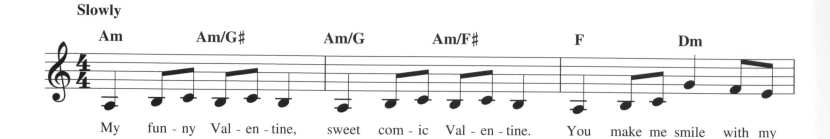

My fun-ny Val-en-tine, sweet com-ic Val-en-tine. You make me smile with my

heart. Your looks are laugh-a-ble, un-pho-to-graph-a-ble,

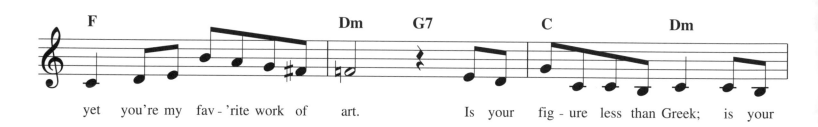

yet you're my fav-'rite work of art. Is your fig-ure less than Greek; is your

mouth a lit-tle weak; when you o-pen it to speak, are you

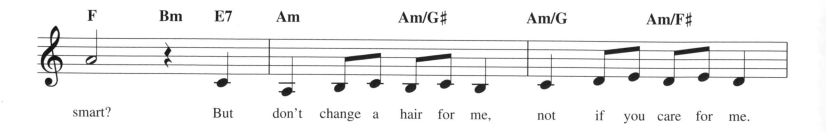

smart? But don't change a hair for me, not if you care for me.

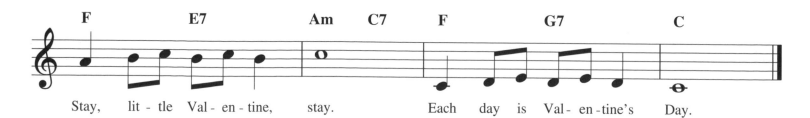

Stay, lit-tle Val-en-tine, stay. Each day is Val-en-tine's Day.

MY HEART BELONGS TO DADDY

from LEAVE IT TO ME

Words and Music by
COLE PORTER

MY OLD FLAME

from the Paramount Picture BELLE OF THE NINETIES

Words and Music by ARTHUR JOHNSTON
and SAM COSLOW

MY ROMANCE

from JUMBO

Words by LORENZ HART
Music by RICHARD RODGERS

MY SILENT LOVE

Words by EDWARD HEYMAN
Music by DANA SUESSE

NEVERTHELESS
(I'm in Love with You)

Words and Music by BERT KALMAR
and HARRY RUBY

THE NEARNESS OF YOU
from the Paramount Picture ROMANCE IN THE DARK

Words by NED WASHINGTON
Music by HOAGY CARMICHAEL

Slow and bluesy

It's not the pale moon that ex-cites me, that thrills and de-lights me. Oh,

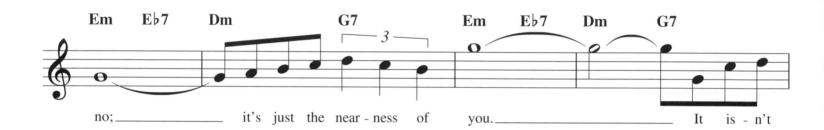

no;_____ it's just the near-ness of you._____ It is-n't

your sweet con-ver-sa-tion that brings this sen-sa-tion. Oh,

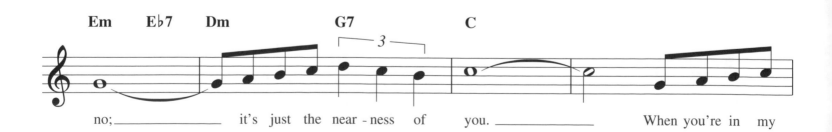

no;_____ it's just the near-ness of you. _____ When you're in my

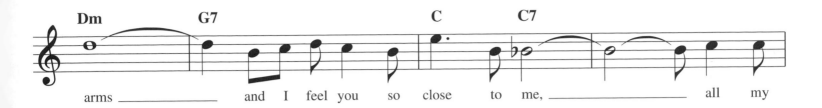

arms _____ and I feel you so close to me, _____ all my

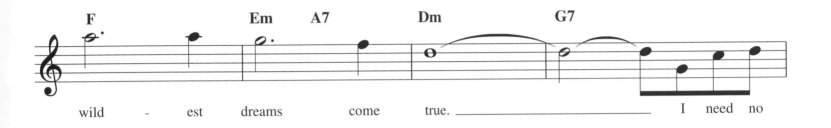

wild - est dreams come true. _____ I need no

soft lights to en - chant me if you'll on - ly grant me the

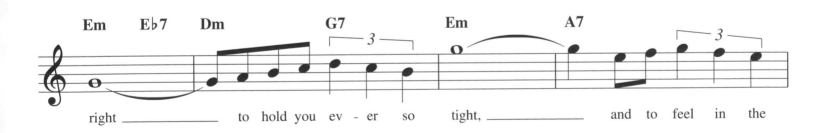

right _____ to hold you ev - er so tight, _____ and to feel in the

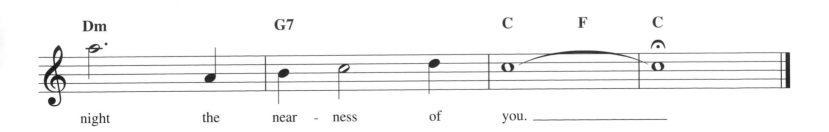

night the near - ness of you. _____

ON THE SUNNY SIDE OF THE STREET

Lyric by DOROTHY FIELDS
Music by JIMMY McHUGH

OUT OF NOWHERE
from the Paramount Picture DUDE RANCH

Words by EDWARD HEYMAN
Music by JOHNNY GREEN

PENNIES FROM HEAVEN
from PENNIES FROM HEAVEN

Words by JOHN BURKE
Music by ARTHUR JOHNSTON

Moderately

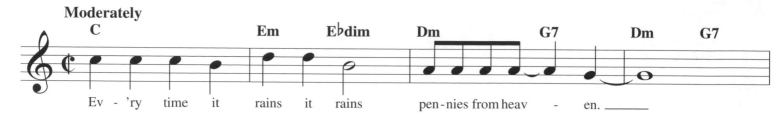

Ev - 'ry time it rains it rains pen-nies from heav - en. _____

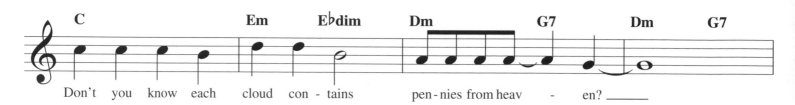

Don't you know each cloud con - tains pen-nies from heav - en? _____

You'll find your for - tune fall - ing all o - ver town.

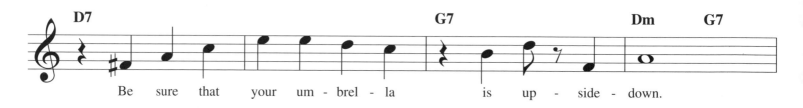

Be sure that your um - brel - la is up - side - down.

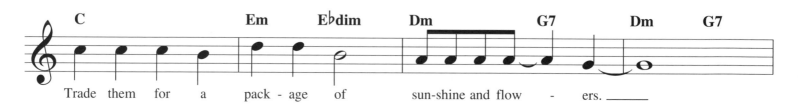

Trade them for a pack - age of sun-shine and flow - ers. _____

If you want the things you love, you must have show - ers. _____

So when you hear it thun - der, don't run un - der a tree, ___ there'll be

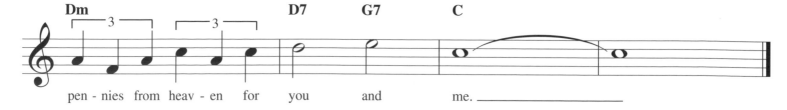

pen - nies from heav - en for you and me. _____

POINCIANA
(Song of the Tree)

Words by BUDDY BERNIER
Music by NAT SIMON

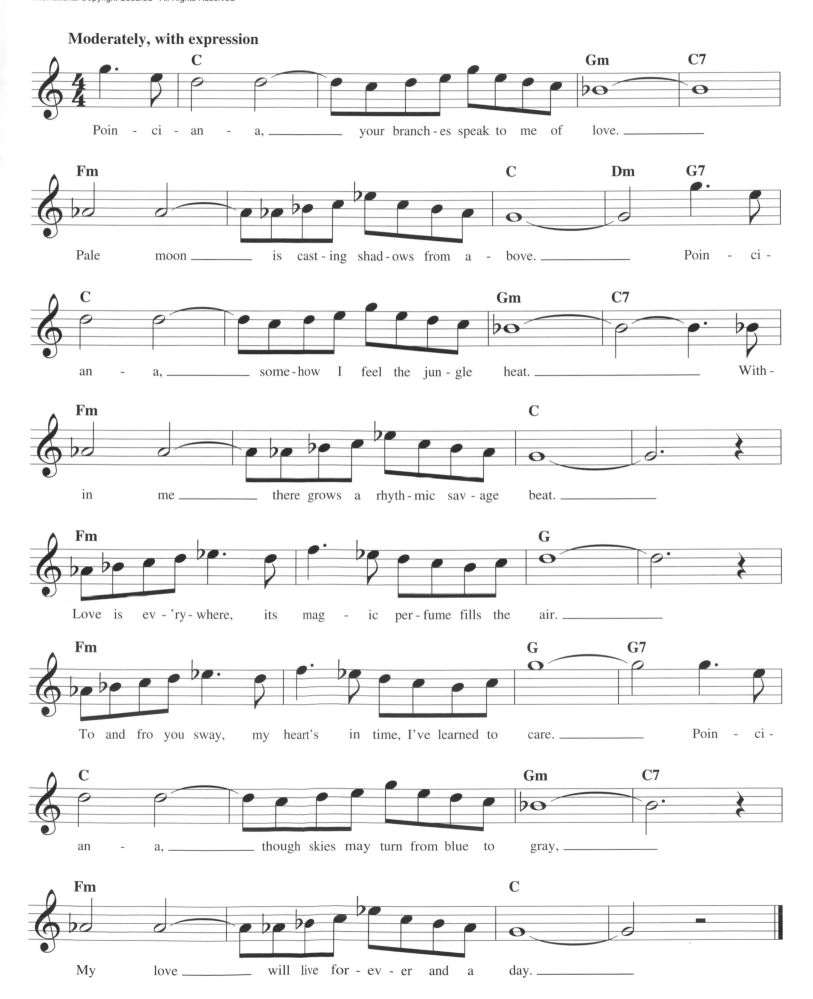

Moderately, with expression

Poin - ci - an - a, _____ your branch - es speak to me of love. _____

Pale moon _____ is cast - ing shad - ows from a - bove. _____ Poin - ci -

an - a, _____ some - how I feel the jun - gle heat. _____ With -

in me _____ there grows a rhyth - mic sav - age beat. _____

Love is ev - 'ry - where, its mag - ic per - fume fills the air. _____

To and fro you sway, my heart's in time, I've learned to care. _____ Poin - ci -

an - a, _____ though skies may turn from blue to gray, _____

My love _____ will live for - ev - er and a day. _____

PUTTIN' ON THE RITZ
from the Motion Picture PUTTIN' ON THE RITZ

Words and Music by
IRVING BERLIN

ROCKIN' CHAIR

Words and Music by
HOAGY CARMICHAEL

SAY IT ISN'T SO

Words and Music by
IRVING BERLIN

SEPTEMBER SONG
from the Musical Play KNICKERBOCKER HOLIDAY

Words by MAXWELL ANDERSON
Music by KURT WEILL

SMALL FRY
from the Paramount Motion Picture SING, YOU SINNERS

Words by FRANK LOESSER
Music by HOAGY CARMICHAEL

Moderate Swing

Small   fry,   strut - tin' by the pool room, small   fry,

should be   in   the school-room.   My,   my,   put   down that cig - a - rette,   you

ain't   a grown - up high and might - y   yet.   Small   fry,

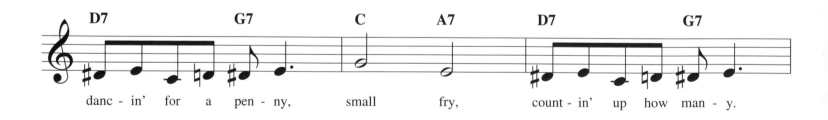

danc - in' for a pen - ny,   small   fry,   count - in' up how man - y.

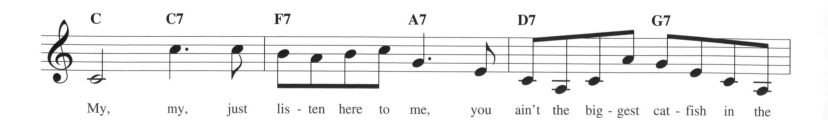

My,   my,   just lis - ten here to me,   you ain't the big - gest cat-fish in the

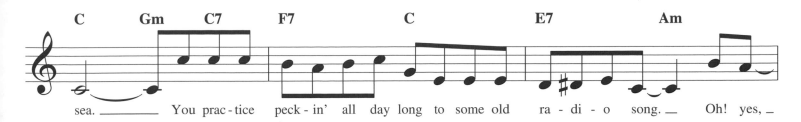

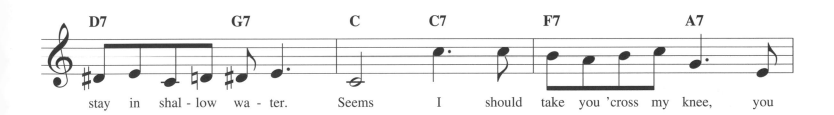

SMOKE GETS IN YOUR EYES
from ROBERTA

Words by OTTO HARBACH
Music by JEROME KERN

SOFT LIGHTS AND SWEET MUSIC
from the Stage Production FACE THE MUSIC

Words and Music by
IRVING BERLIN

SOMEBODY ELSE IS TAKING MY PLACE

Words and Music by DICK HOWARD,
BOB ELLSWORTH and RUSS MORGAN

Slowly, with expression

STOMPIN' AT THE SAVOY

Words by ANDY RAZAF
Music by BENNY GOODMAN,
EDGAR SAMPSON and CHICK WEBB

THE SONG IS YOU
from MUSIC IN THE AIR

Lyrics by OSCAR HAMMERSTEIN II
Music by JEROME KERN

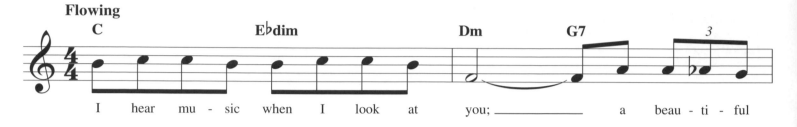

I hear mu - sic when I look at you; _____ a beau - ti - ful

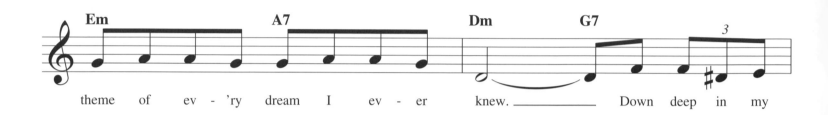

theme of ev - 'ry dream I ev - er knew. _____ Down deep in my

heart _____ I hear it play. _____ I feel it

start, _____ then melt a - way. I hear mu - sic when I touch your

hand; _____ a beau - ti - ful mel - o - dy from some en - chant - ed

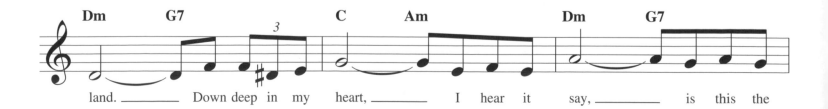

land. _____ Down deep in my heart, _____ I hear it say, _____ is this the

115

STARDUST

Words by MITCHELL PARISH
Music by HOAGY CARMICHAEL

Moderately

...And now the pur -ple dusk of twi -light time   steals a -cross the mead -ows of my

heart.   High up in the sky the lit - tle stars climb,

al - ways re -mind -ing me that we're a - part.   You wan -dered down the lane and

far a - way,   leav -ing me a song that will not   die.

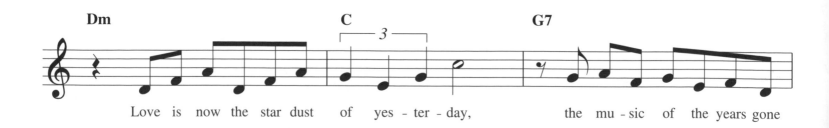

Love is now the star dust of yes -ter -day,   the mu -sic of the years gone

117

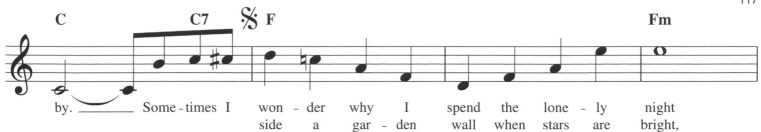

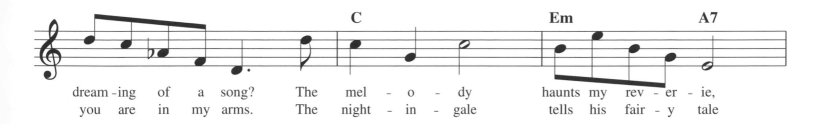

by. _____ Some-times I won-der why I spend the lone-ly night
side a gar-den wall when stars are bright,

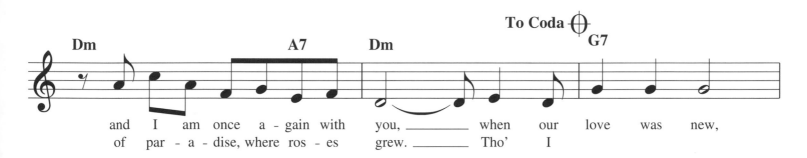

dream-ing of a song? The mel-o-dy haunts my rev-er-ie,
you are in my arms. The night-in-gale tells his fair-y tale

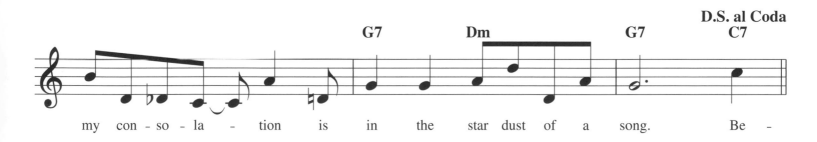

and I am once a-gain with you, _____ when our love was new,
of par-a-dise, where ros-es grew. _____ Tho' I

and each kiss an in-spi-ra - tion. _____ But that was long a-go: now

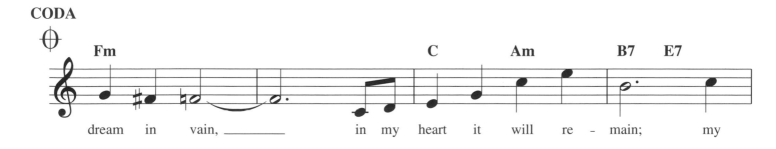

my con-so-la - tion is in the star dust of a song. Be -

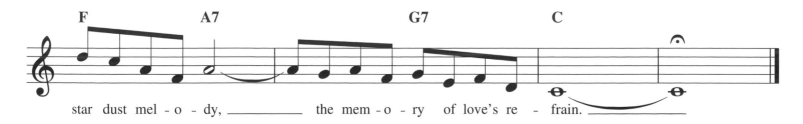

dream in vain, _____ in my heart it will re-main; my
star dust mel-o-dy, _____ the mem-o-ry of love's re-frain. _____

STORMY WEATHER
(Keeps Rainin' All the Time)

Lyric by TED KOEHLER
Music by HAROLD ARLEN

Slow lament

Don't know why there's no sun up in the sky, storm - y
bare, gloom and mis - 'ry ev - 'ry - where, storm - y

weath - er. _____ Since my man and I ain't to - geth - er, _____
weath - er. _____ Just can't get my poor self to - geth - er. _____

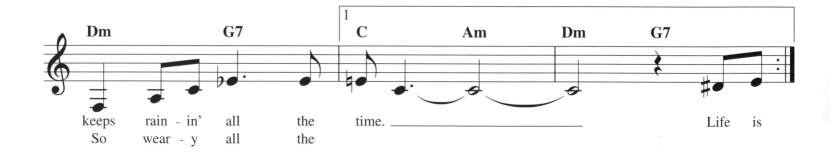

keeps rain - in' all the time. _____
So wear - y all the

Life is

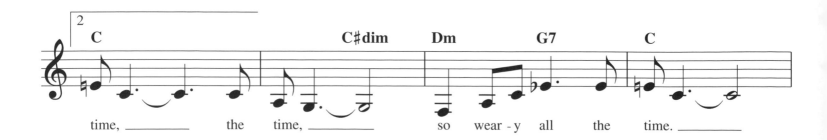

time, _____ the time, _____ so wear - y all the time. _____

When he went a-way the blues walked in and met me. If he stays a-way old rock-in'

chair will get me. All I do is pray the Lord a-bove will let me

walk in the sun once more. Can't go on, ev-'ry-thing I had is gone, storm-y

weath-er._____ Since my man and I ain't to-geth-er,_____ keeps rain-in' all the

time _____ keeps rain-in' all the time. _____

THANKS FOR THE MEMORY
from the Paramount Picture BIG BROADCAST OF 1938

Words and Music by LEO ROBIN
and RALPH RAINGER

Moderately

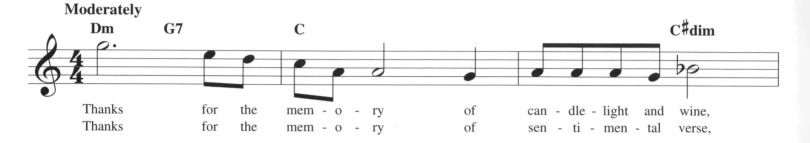

Thanks for the mem - o - ry of can - dle - light and wine,
Thanks for the mem - o - ry of sen - ti - men - tal verse,

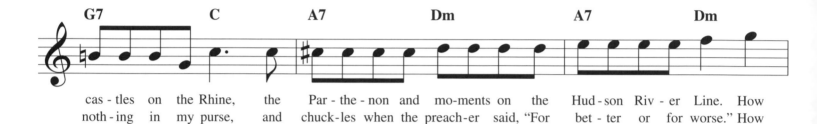

cas - tles on the Rhine, the Par - the - non and mo - ments on the Hud - son Riv - er Line. How
noth - ing in my purse, and chuck - les when the preach - er said, "For bet - ter or for worse." How

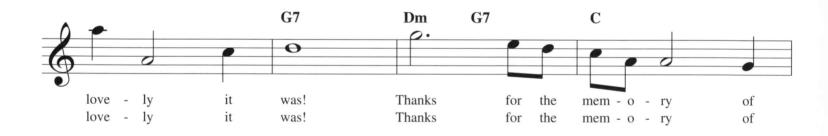

love - ly it was! Thanks for the mem - o - ry of
love - ly it was! Thanks for the mem - o - ry of

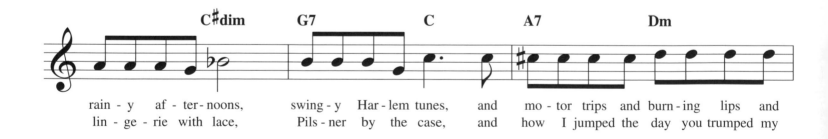

rain - y af - ter - noons, swing - y Har - lem tunes, and mo - tor trips and burn - ing lips and
lin - ge - rie with lace, Pils - ner by the case, and how I jumped the day you trumped my

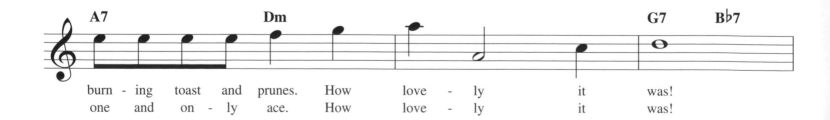

burn - ing toast and prunes. How love - ly it was!
one and on - ly ace. How love - ly it was!

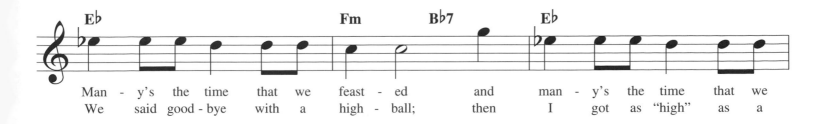

Man - y's the time that we feast - ed and man - y's the time that we
We said good - bye with a high - ball; then I got as "high" as a

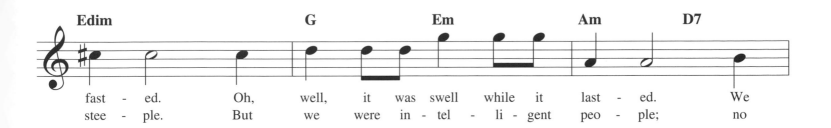

fast - ed. Oh, well, it was swell while it last - ed. We
stee - ple. But we were in - tel - li - gent peo - ple; no

did have fun and no harm done. And thanks for the mem - o - ry of
tears, no fuss, hur - ray for us. So thanks for the mem - o - ry and

sun - burns at the shore, nights in Sing - a - pore. You might have been a head - ache but you
strict - ly en - tre - nous, dar - ling, how are you? And how are all the lit - tle dreams that

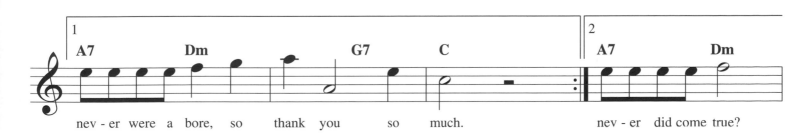

nev - er were a bore, so thank you so much.
nev - er did come true?

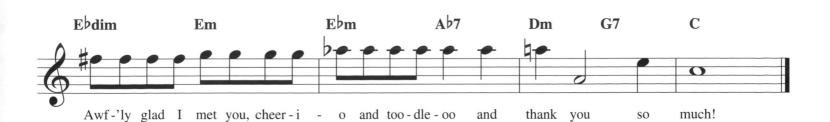

Awf - 'ly glad I met you, cheer - i - o and too - dle - oo and thank you so much!

THERE IS NO GREATER LOVE

Words by MARTY SYMES
Music by ISHAM JONES

THERE'S A SMALL HOTEL
from ON YOUR TOES

Words by LORENZ HART
Music by RICHARD RODGERS

THIS CAN'T BE LOVE
from THE BOYS FROM SYRACUSE

Words by LORENZ HART
Music by RICHARD RODGERS

Moderately, smoothly

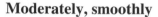

This can't be love be-cause I feel so well, _____ no

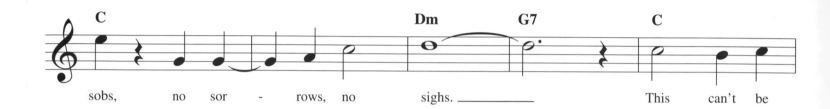

sobs, no sor - rows, no sighs. _____ This can't be

love, I get no diz - zy spell _____ my head is not _____

_____ in the skies. _____ My heart does not stand still, _____

_____ just hear it beat! This is too sweet to

be love. This can't be love be - cause I feel so well; _____

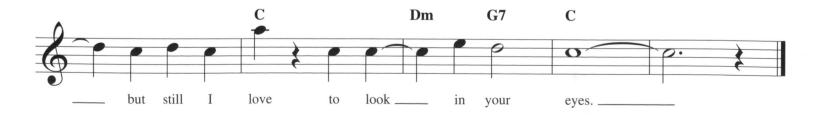

_____ but still I love to look _____ in your eyes. _____

TWO SLEEPY PEOPLE
from the Paramount Motion Picture THANKS FOR THE MEMORY

Words by FRANK LOESSER
Music by HOAGY CARMICHAEL

THE VERY THOUGHT OF YOU

Words and Music by
RAY NOBLE

WHAT A DIFF'RENCE A DAY MADE

English Words by STANLEY ADAMS
Music and Spanish Words by MARIA GREVER

THE WAY YOU LOOK TONIGHT
from SWING TIME

Words by DOROTHY FIELDS
Music by JEROME KERN

Moderately

Some - day when I'm aw - f'ly low,
love - ly, with your smile so warm
Love - ly, nev - er, nev - er change,

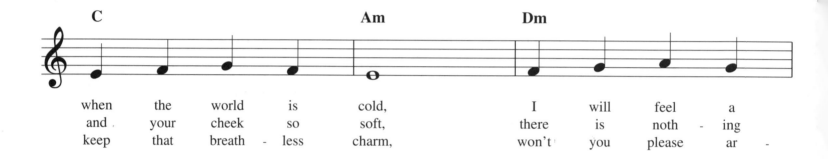

when the world is cold, I will feel a
and your cheek so soft, there is noth - ing
keep that breath - less charm, won't you please ar -

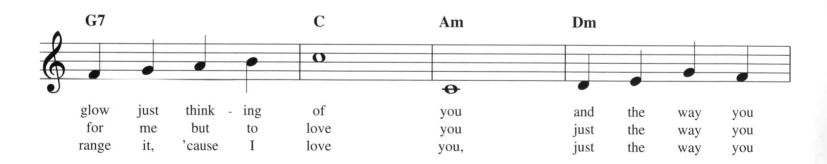

glow just think - ing of you and the way you
for me but to love you just the way you
range it, 'cause I love you, just the way you

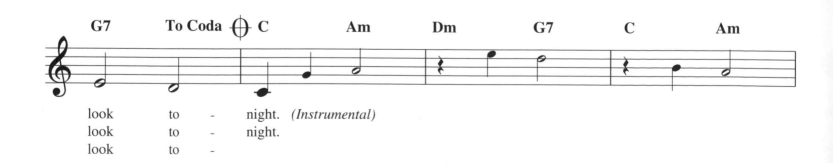

look to - night. *(Instrumental)*
look to - night.
look to -

129

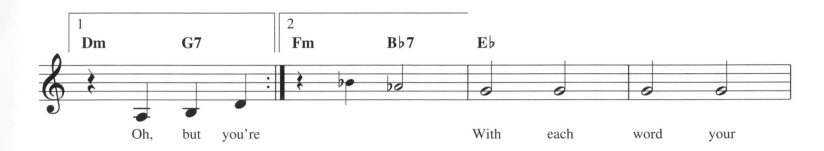

1 **Dm** **G7** 2 **Fm** **Bb7** **Eb**

Oh, but you're With each word your

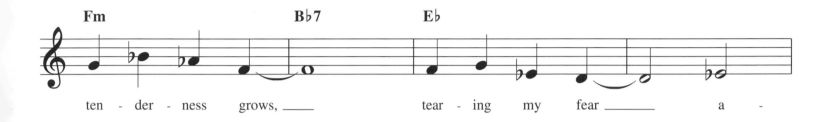

Fm **Bb7** **Eb**

ten - der - ness grows, _____ tear - ing my fear _____ a -

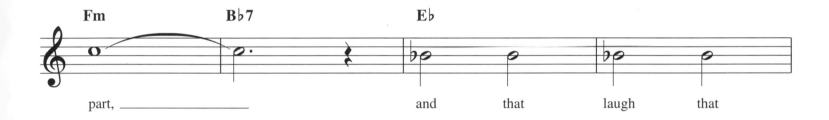

Fm **Bb7** **Eb**

part, _____ and that laugh that

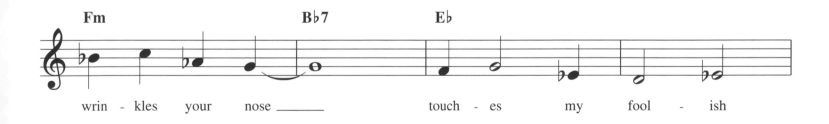

Fm **Bb7** **Eb**

wrin - kles your nose _____ touch - es my fool - ish

Dm **G7** **D.C. al Coda**

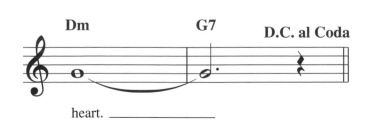

heart. _____

CODA

C

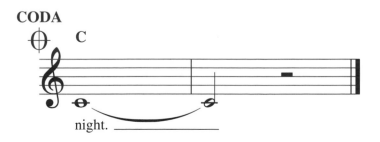

night. _____

WHAT'S NEW?

Words by JOHNNY BURKE
Music by BOB HAGGART

WHERE OR WHEN
from BABES IN ARMS

Words by LORENZ HART
Music by RICHARD RODGERS

WRAP YOUR TROUBLES IN DREAMS
(And Dream Your Troubles Away)

Lyric by TED KOEHLER and BILLY MOLL
Music by HARRY BARRIS

YESTERDAYS
from ROBERTA

Words by OTTO HARBACH
Music by JEROME KERN

Slowly

Yes - ter - days, yes - ter - days, days I knew as hap - py, sweet se -

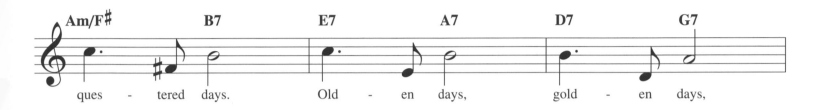

ques - tered days. Old - en days, gold - en days,

days of mad ro - mance and love. Then gay youth was mine,

truth was mine, joy - ous, free and flam - ing life, for - sooth, was mine.

Sad am I, glad am I for to - day I'm dream - ing

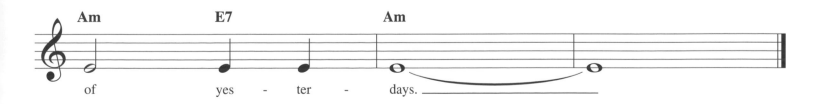

of yes - ter - days.

YOU ARE MY SUNSHINE

Words and Music by
JIMMIE DAVIS

YOU BROUGHT A NEW KIND OF LOVE TO ME
from the Paramount Picture THE BIG POND

Words and Music by SAMMY FAIN,
IRVING KAHAL and PIERRE NORMAN

CHORD SPELLER

C chords

C	C–E–G
Cm	C–E♭–G
C7	C–E–G–B♭
Cdim	C–E♭–G♭
C+	C–E–G♯

C♯ or D♭ chords

C♯	C♯–F–G♯
C♯m	C♯–E–G♯
C♯7	C♯–F– G♯–B
C♯dim	C♯–E–G
C♯+	C♯–F–A

D chords

D	D–F♯–A
Dm	D–F–A
D7	D–F♯–A–C
Ddim	D–F–A♭
D+	D–F♯–A♯

E♭ chords

E♭	E♭–G–B♭
E♭m	E♭–G♭–B♭
E♭7	E♭–G–B♭–D♭
E♭dim	E♭–G♭–A
E♭+	E♭–G–B

E chords

E	E–G♯–B
Em	E–G–B
E7	E–G♯–B–D
Edim	E–G–B♭
E+	E–G♯–C

F chords

F	F–A–C
Fm	F–A♭–C
F7	F–A–C–E♭
Fdim	F–A♭–B
F+	F–A–C♯

F♯ or G♭ chords

F♯	F♯–A♯–C♯
F♯m	F♯–A–C♯
F♯7	F♯–A♯–C♯–E
F♯dim	F♯–A–C
F♯+	F♯–A♯–D

G chords

G	G–B–D
Gm	G–B♭–D
G7	G–B–D–F
Gdim	G–B♭–D♭
G+	G–B–D♯

G♯ or A♭ chords

A♭	A♭–C–E♭
A♭m	A♭–B–E♭
A♭7	A♭–C–E♭–G♭
A♭dim	A♭–B–D
A♭+	A♭–C–E

A chords

A	A–C♯–E
Am	A–C–E
A7	A–C♯–E–G
Adim	A–C–E♭
A+	A–C♯–F

B♭ chords

B♭	B♭–D–F
B♭m	B♭–D♭–F
B♭7	B♭–D–F–A♭
B♭dim	B♭–D♭–E
B♭+	B♭–D–F♯

B chords

B	B–D♯–F♯
Bm	B–D–F♯
B7	B–D♯–F♯–A
Bdim	B–D–F
B+	B–D♯–G

Important Note: A slash chord (C/E, G/B) tells you that a certain bass note is to be played under a particular harmony. In the case of C/E, the chord is C and the bass note is E.